Come Colour Me In

Illustrated By
©Peter Maddocks 2015

Published By
Peter Maddocks & Marian Bonelli

http://petermaddocksart.com/
PublishedByMe.blogspot.com
ISBN-13:978-1512389722
ISBN-10:1512389722

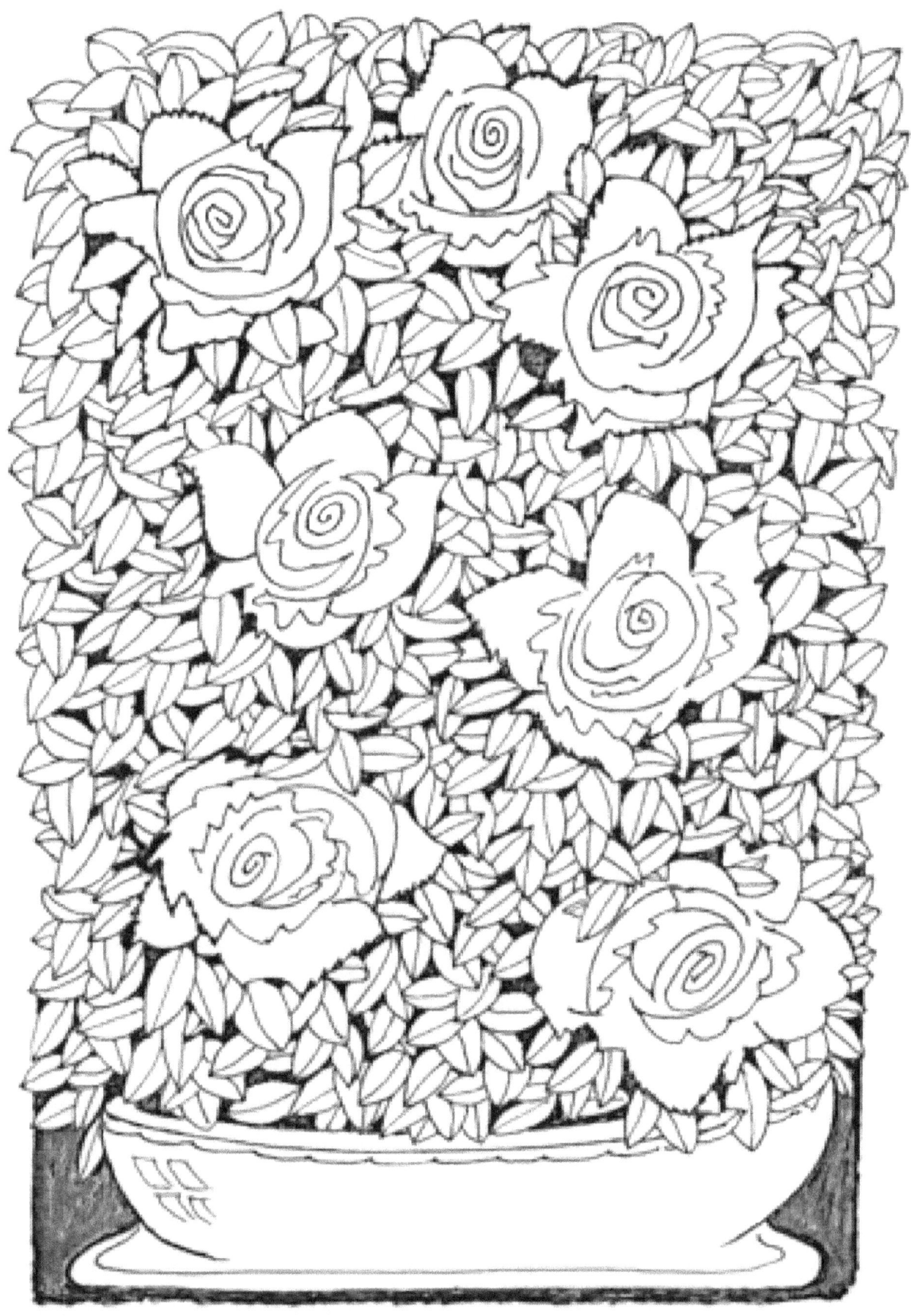

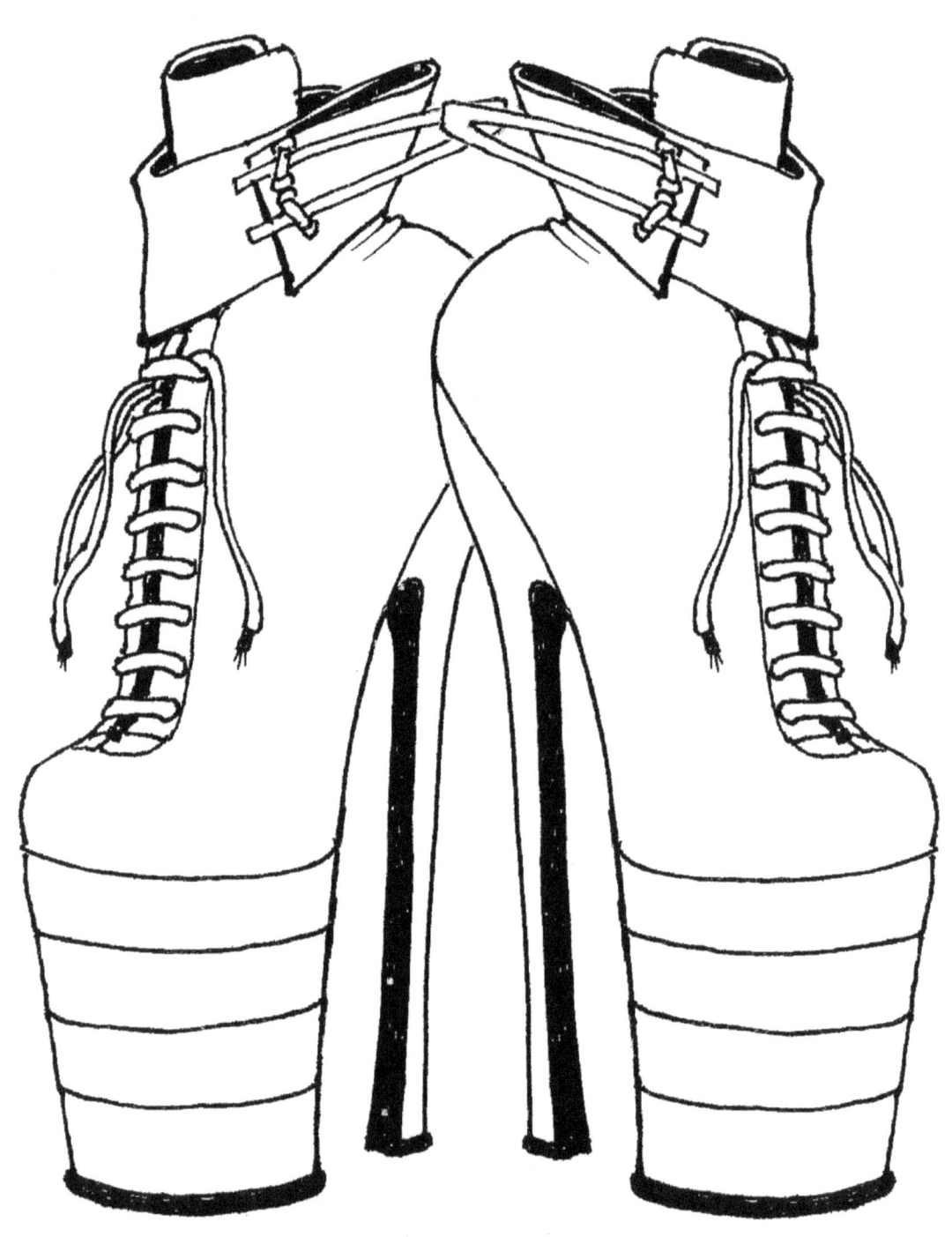

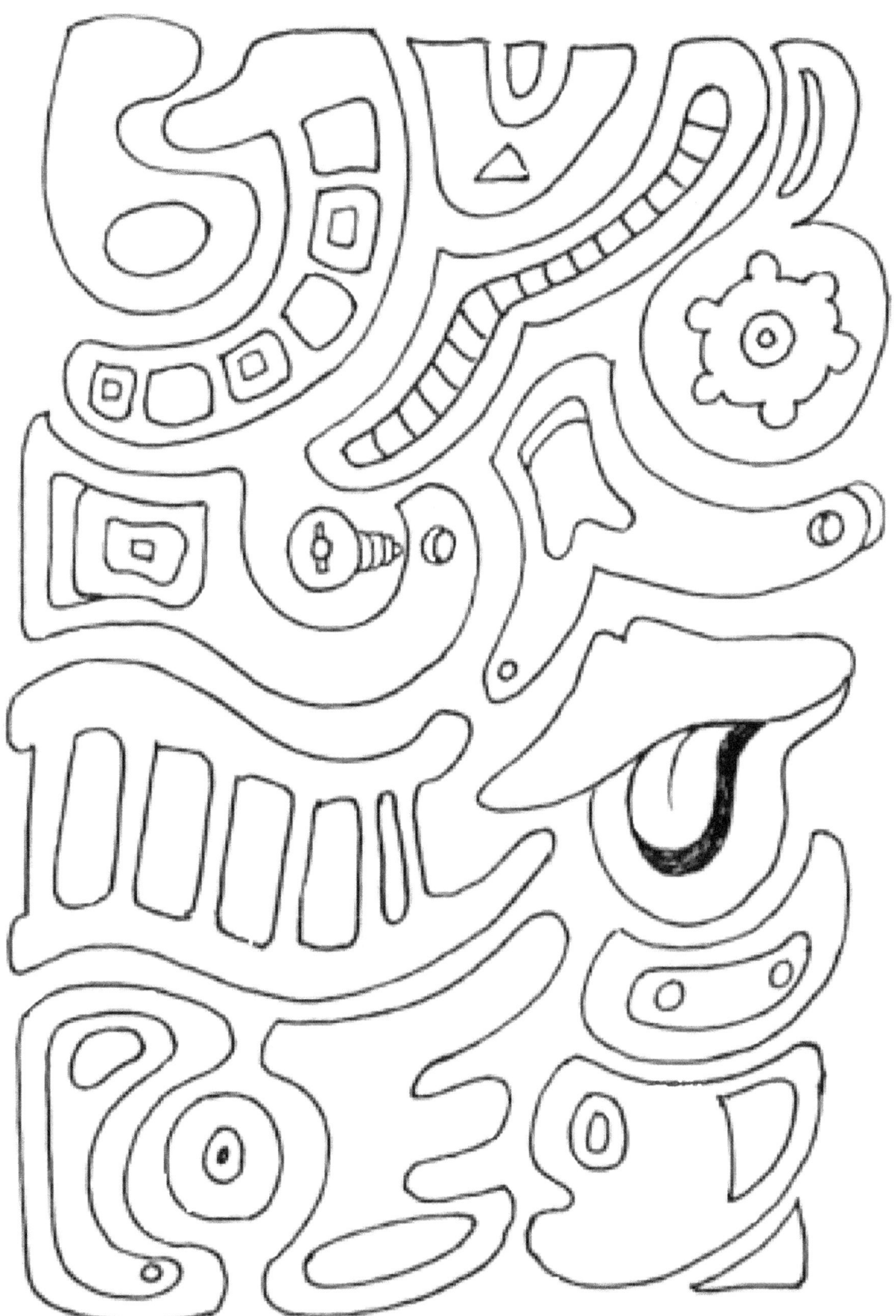

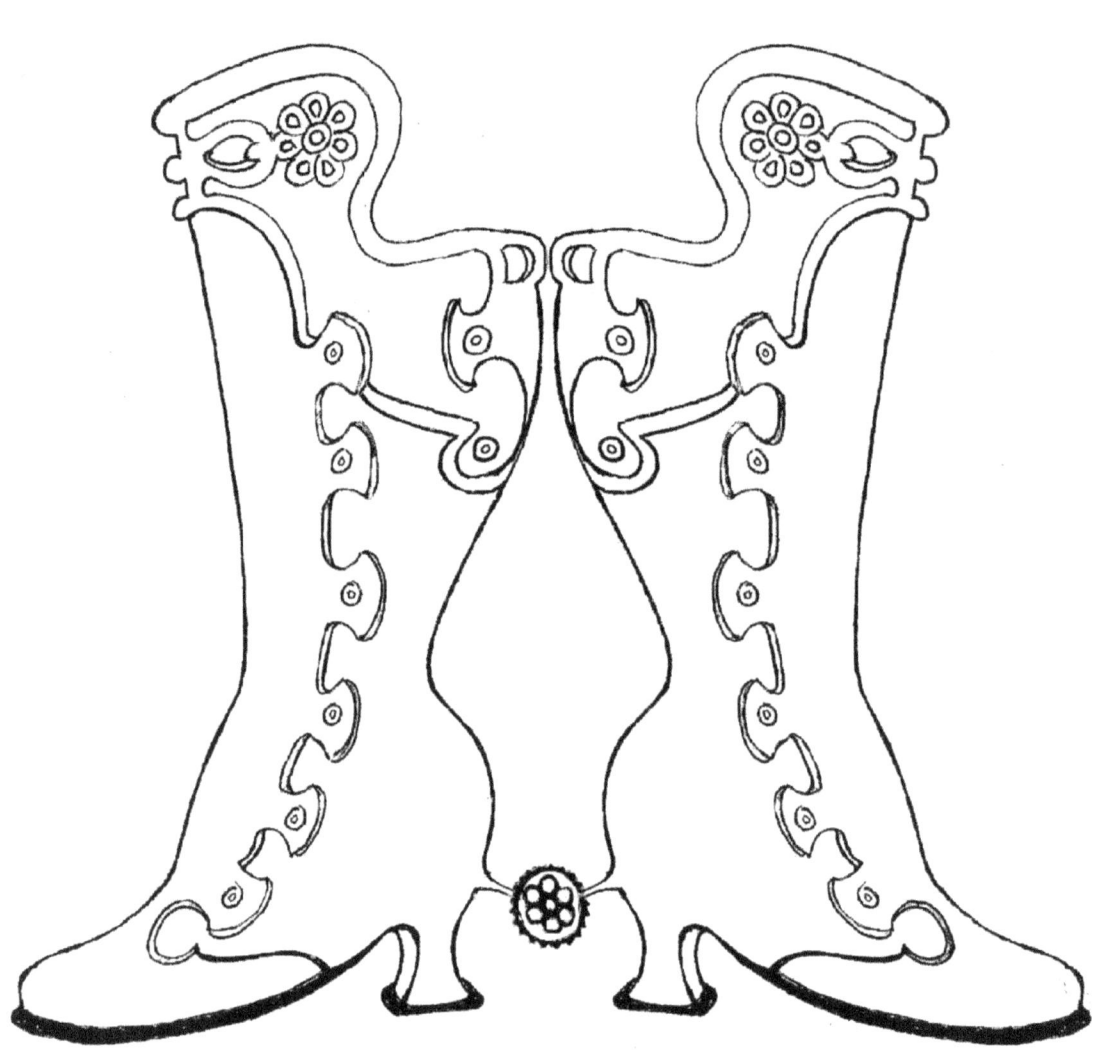

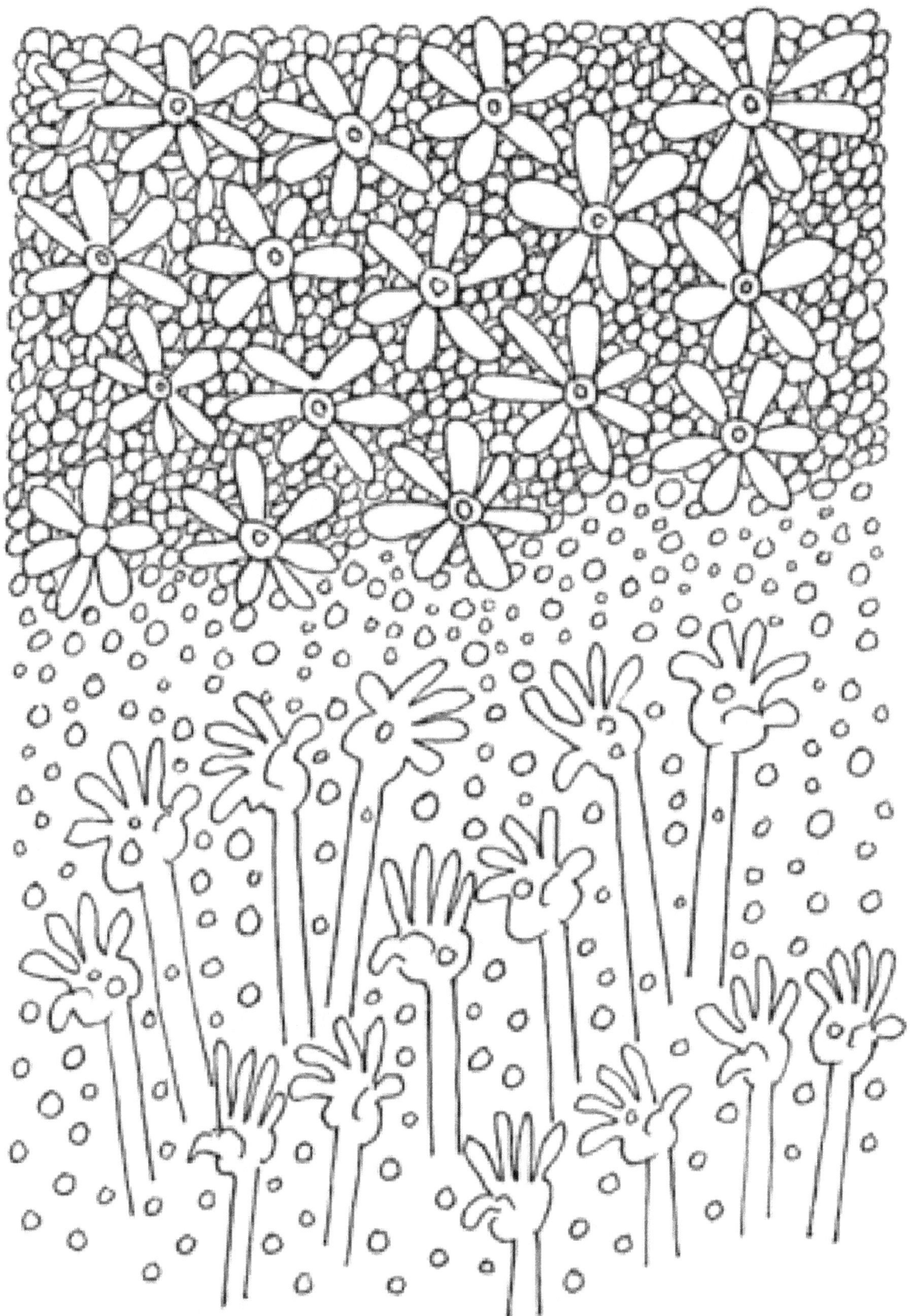

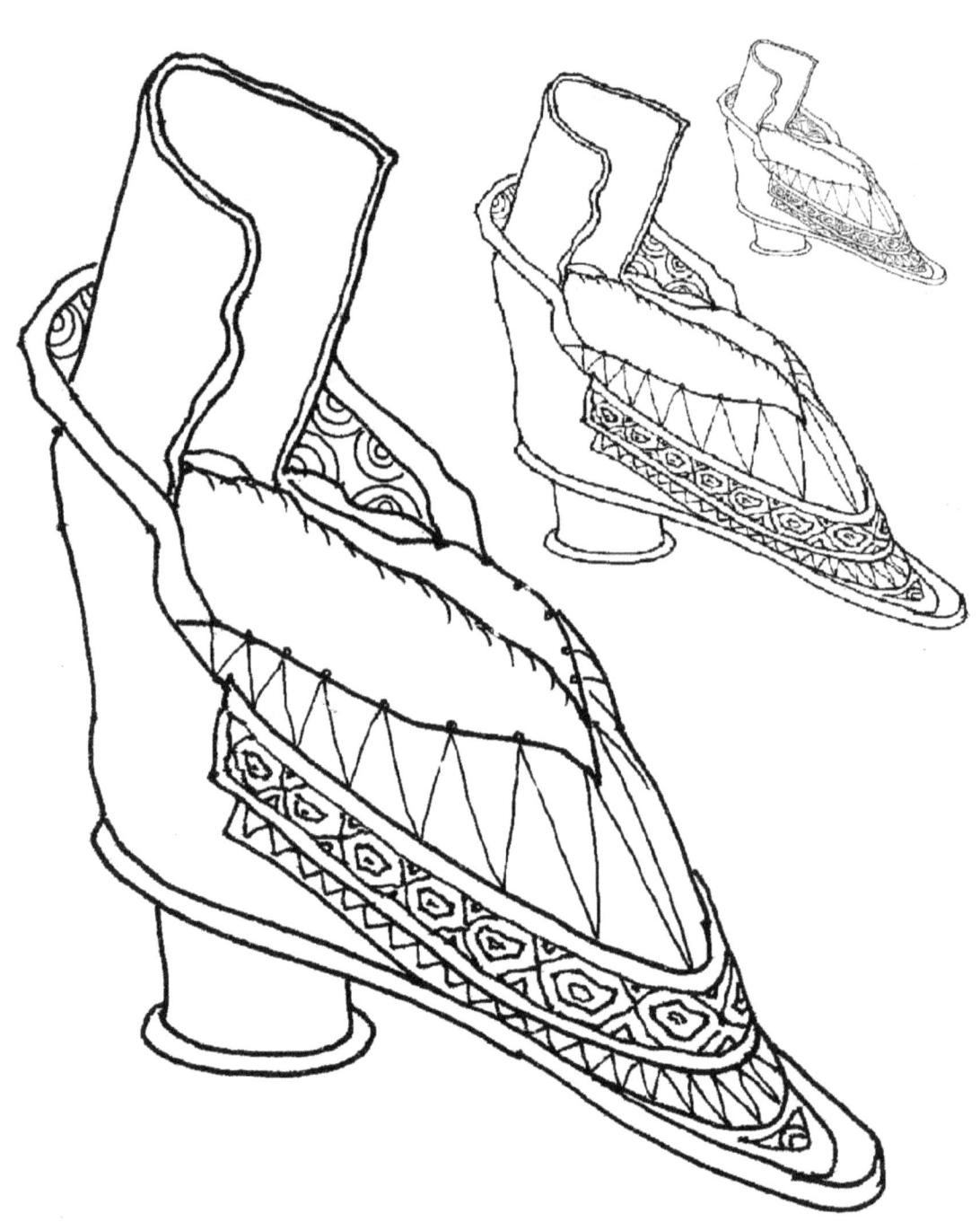

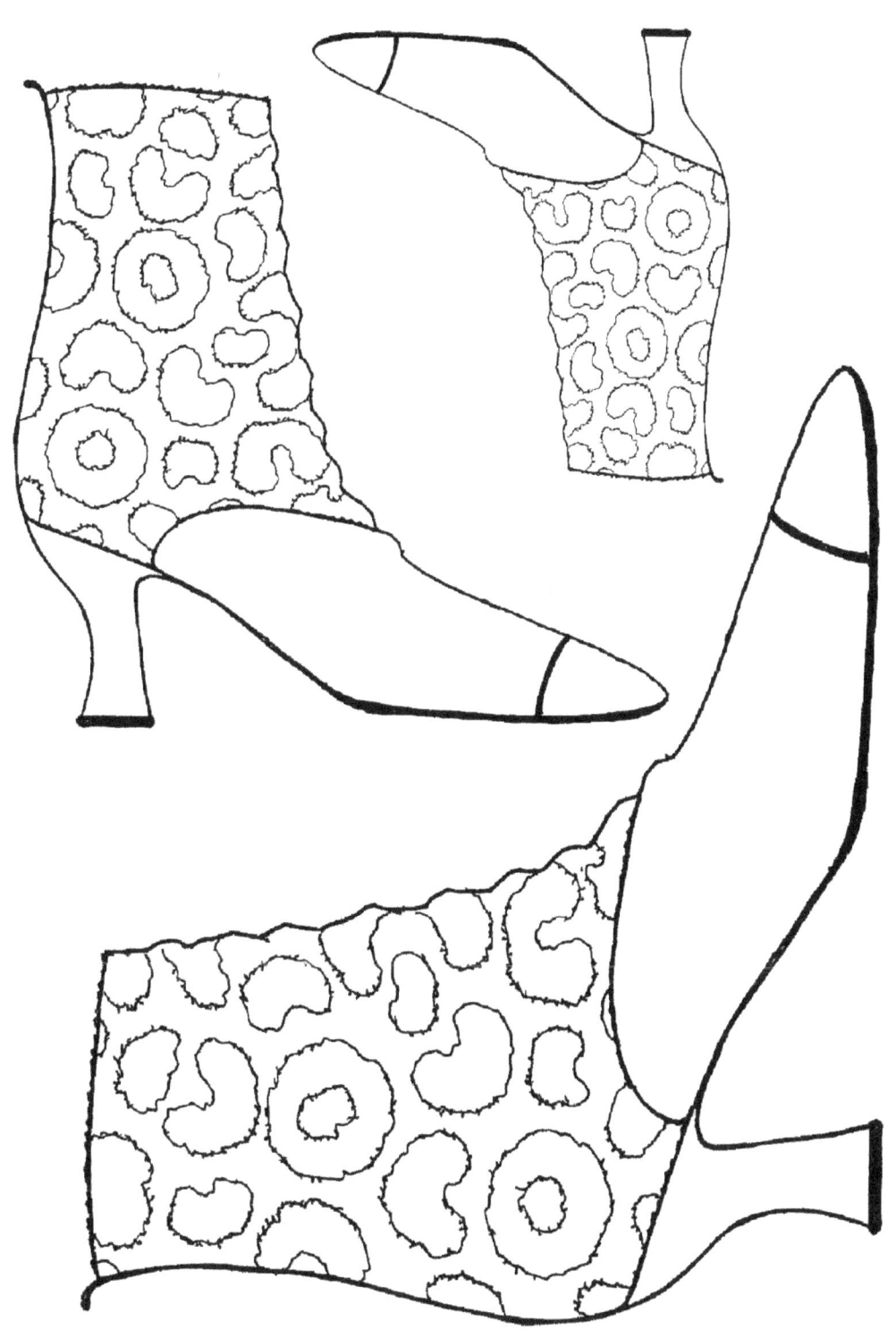

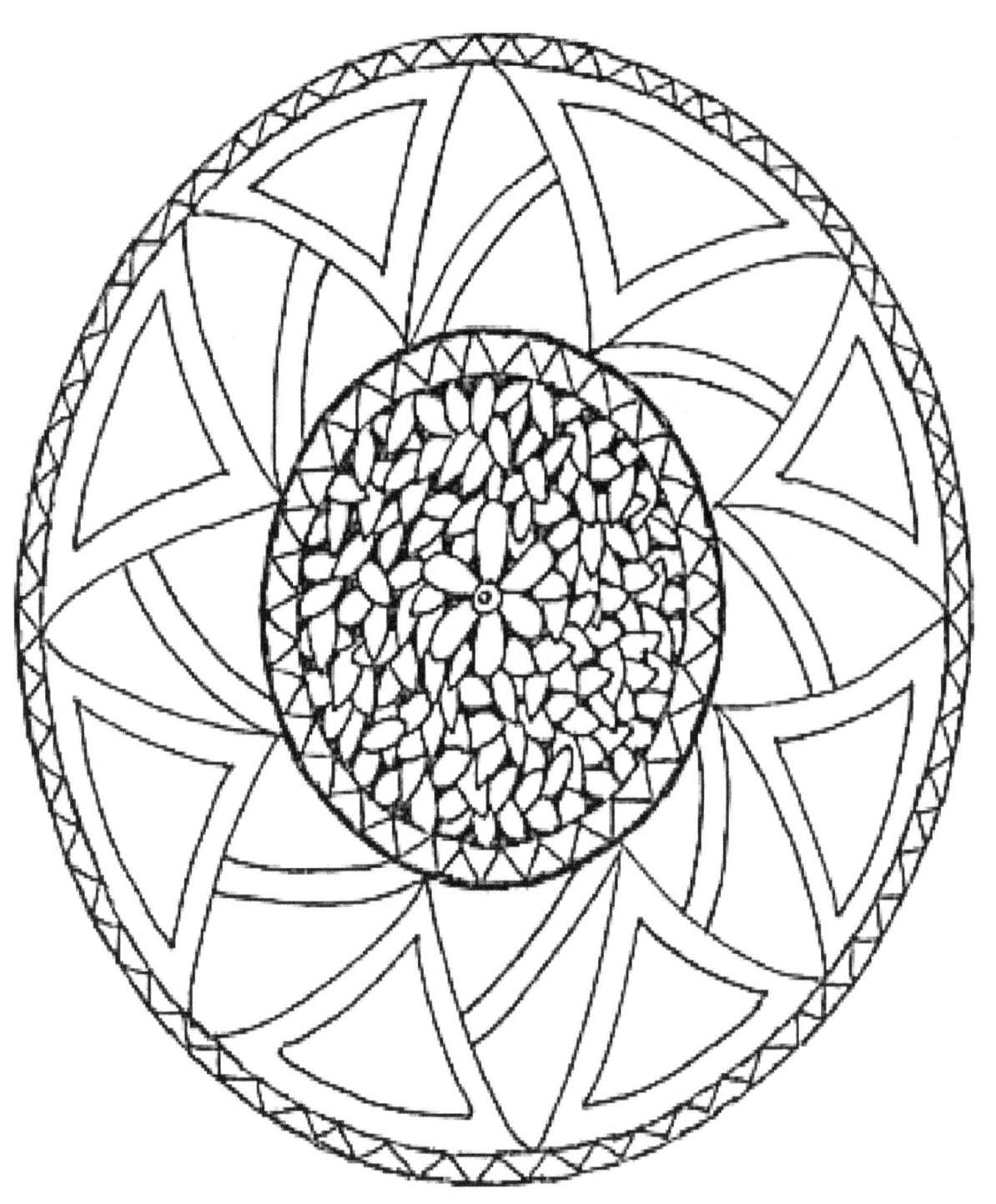

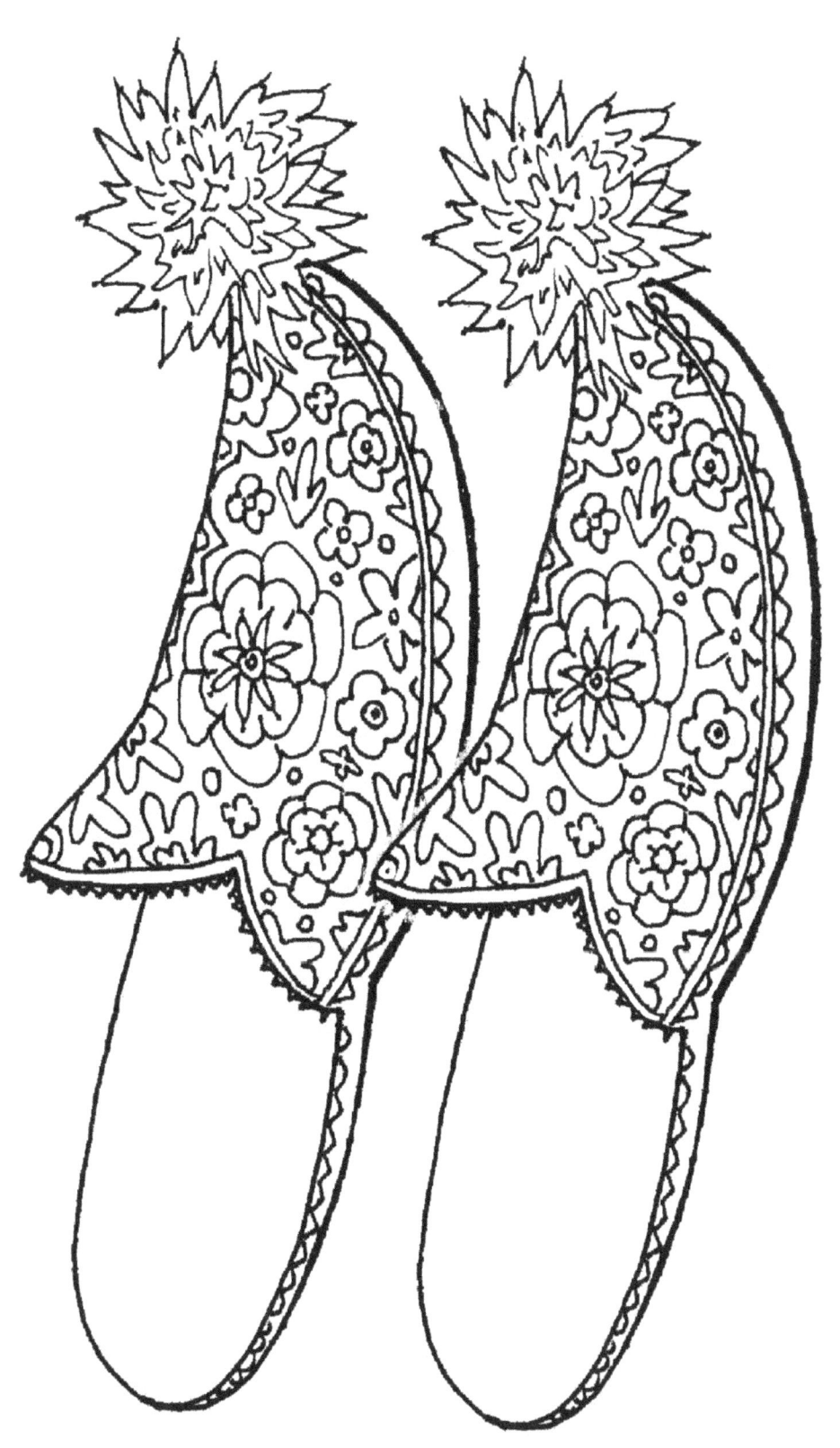

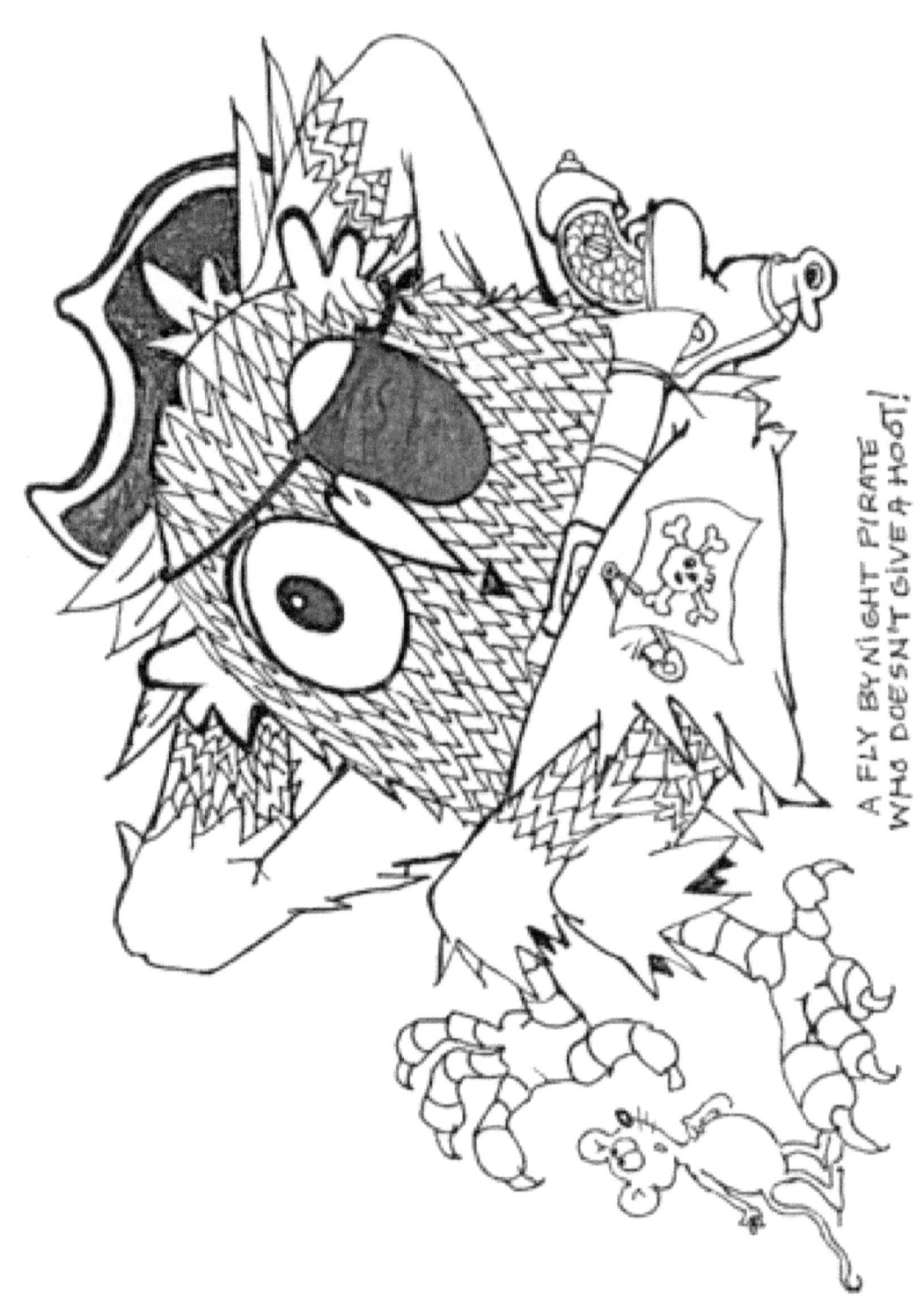

A FLY BY NIGHT PIRATE WHO DOESN'T GIVE A HOOT!

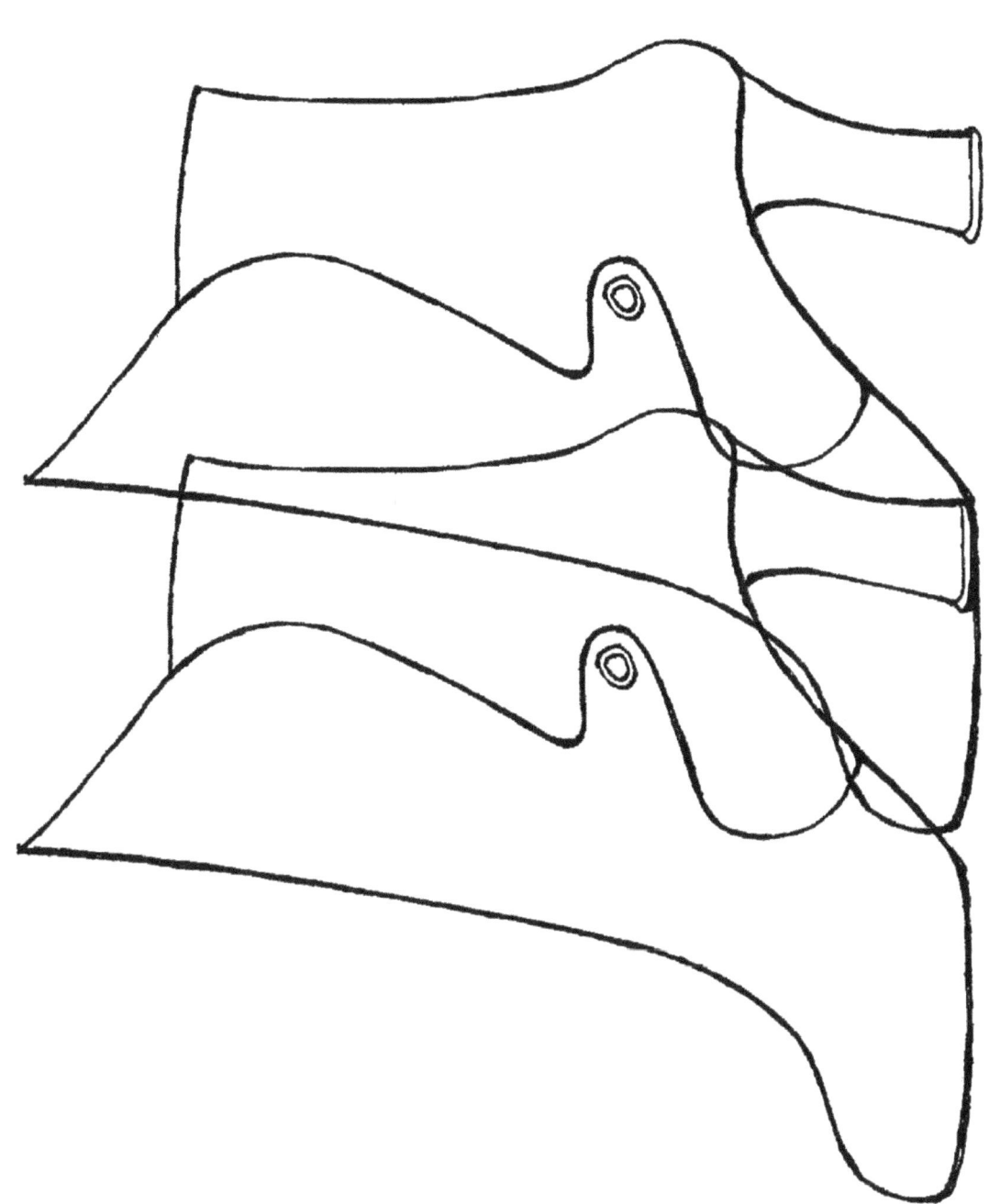

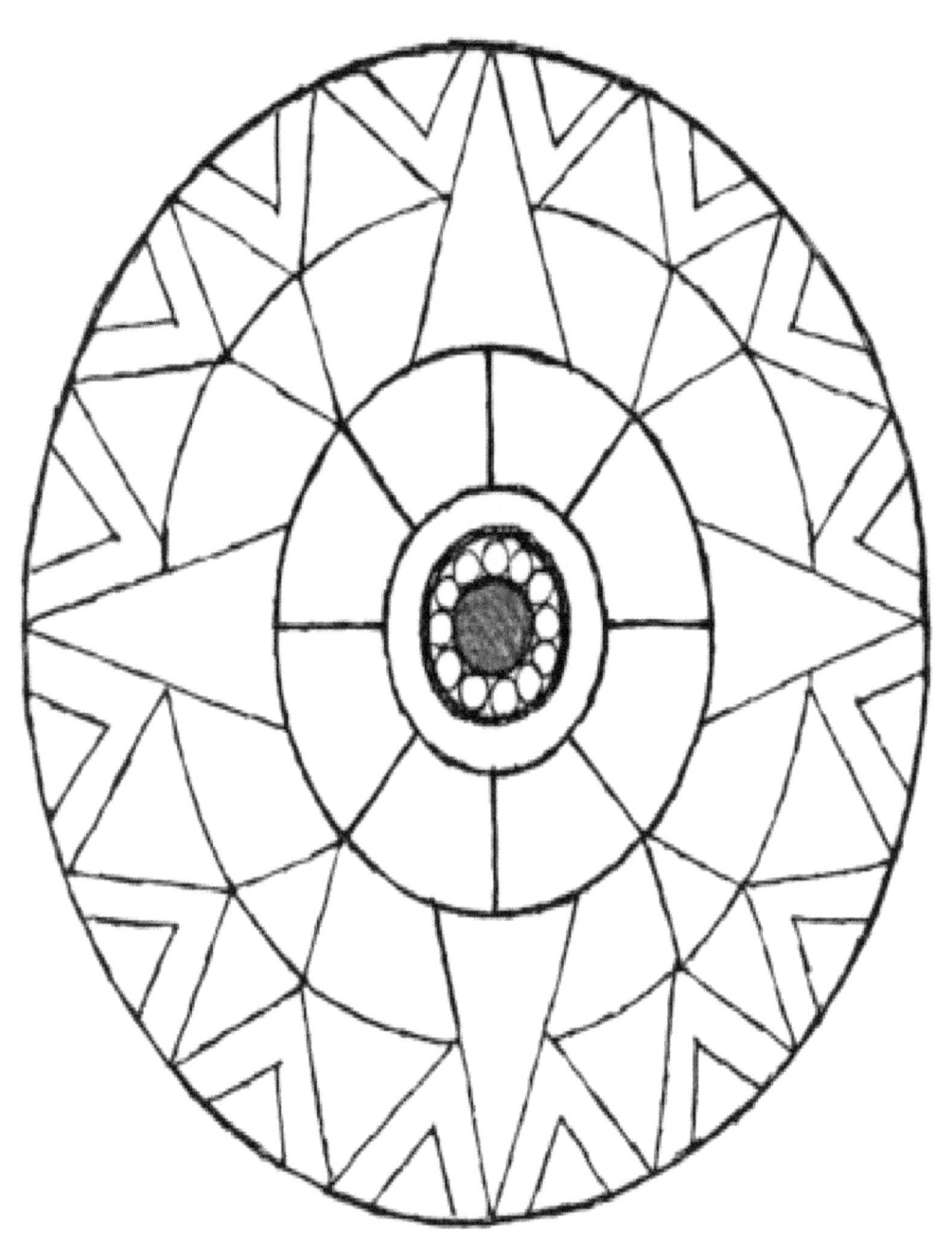

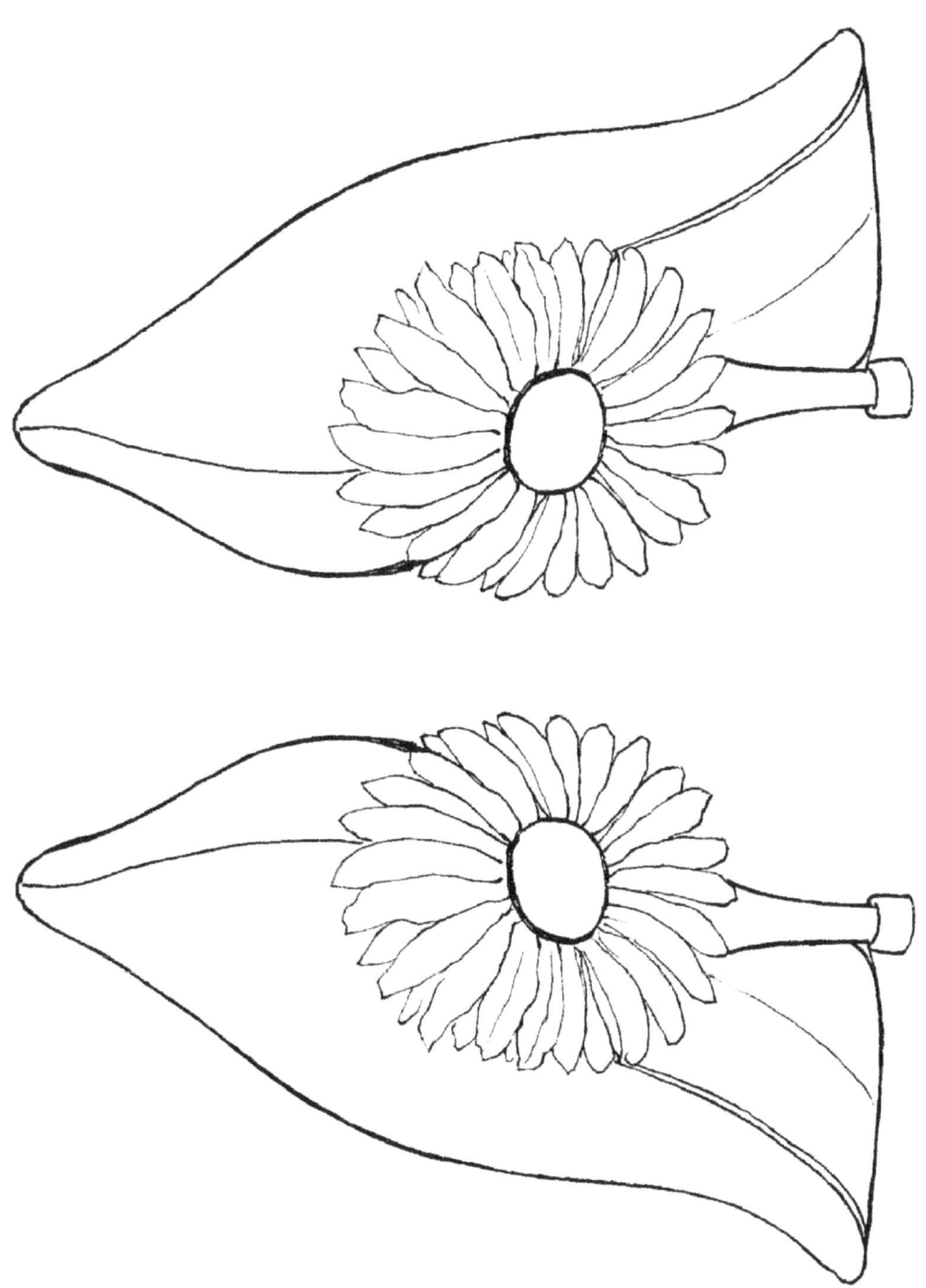

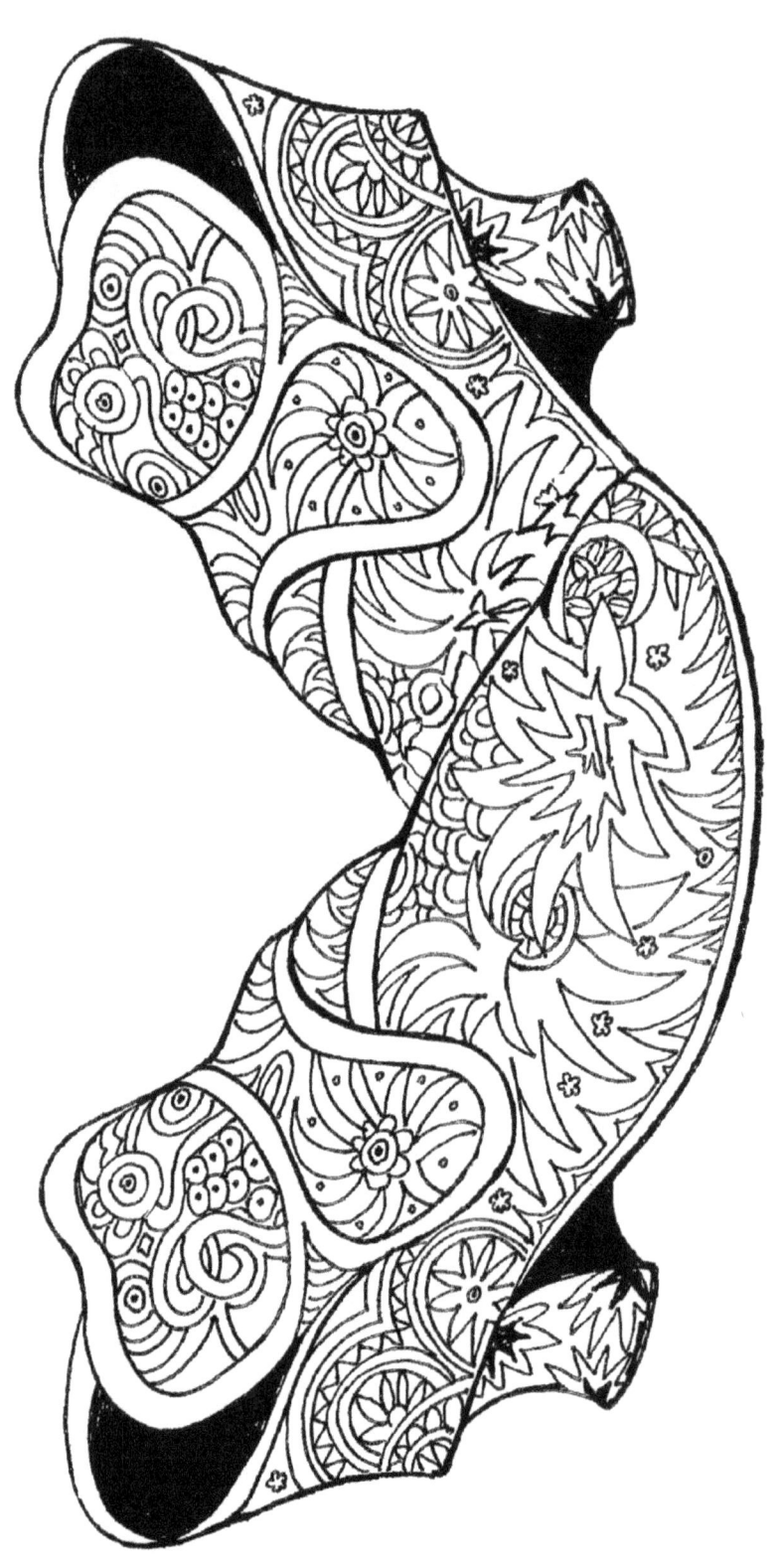

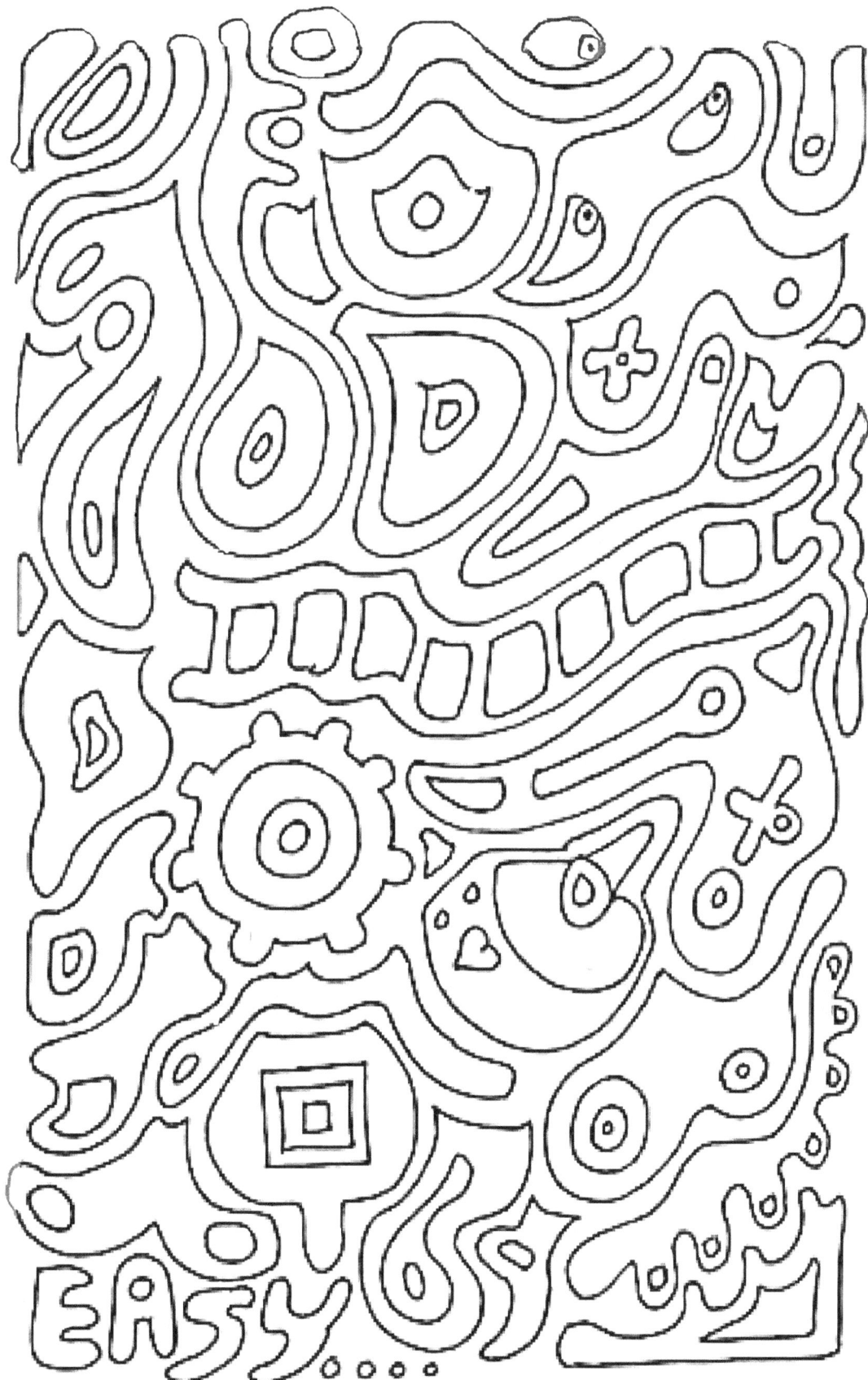

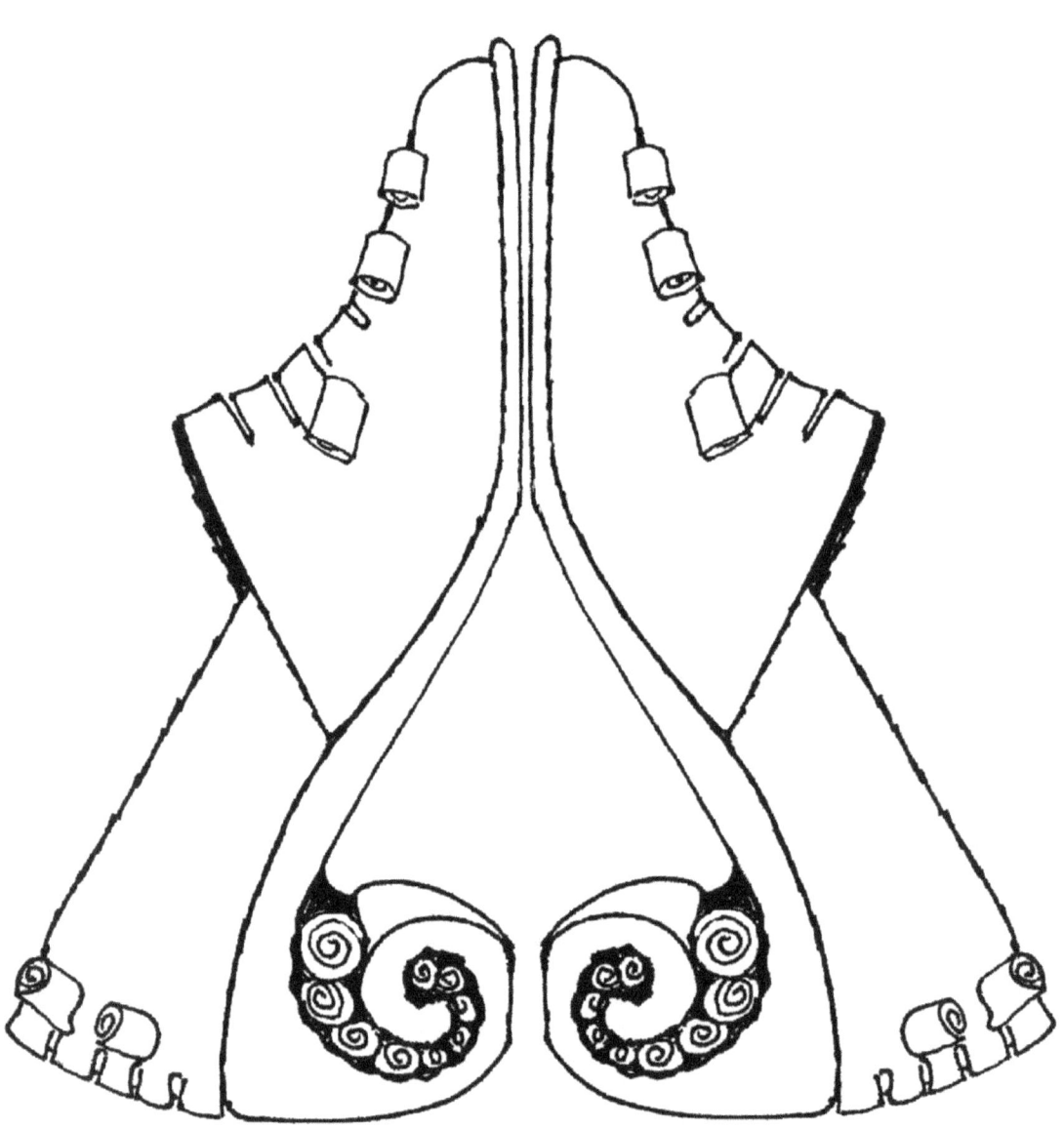

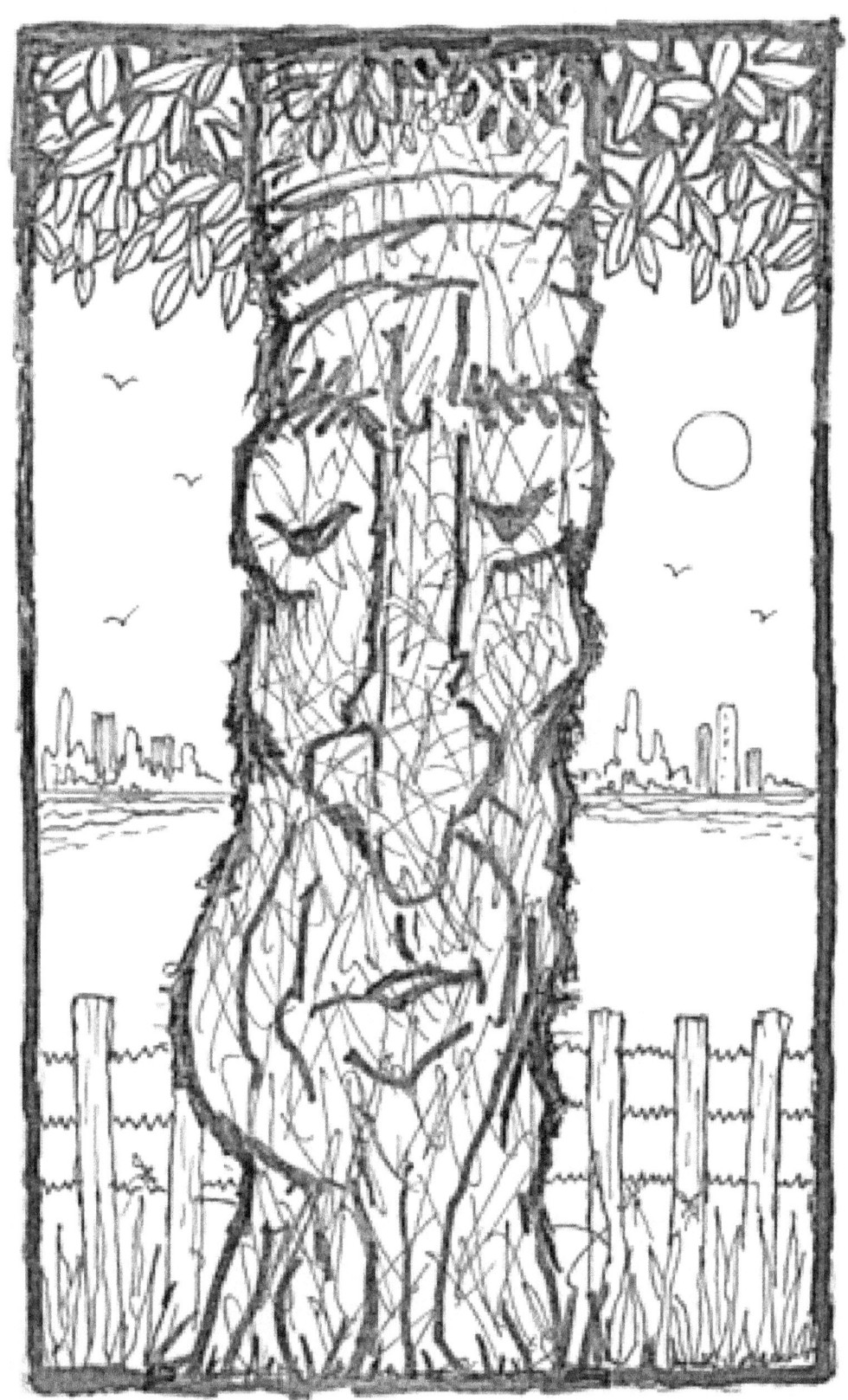

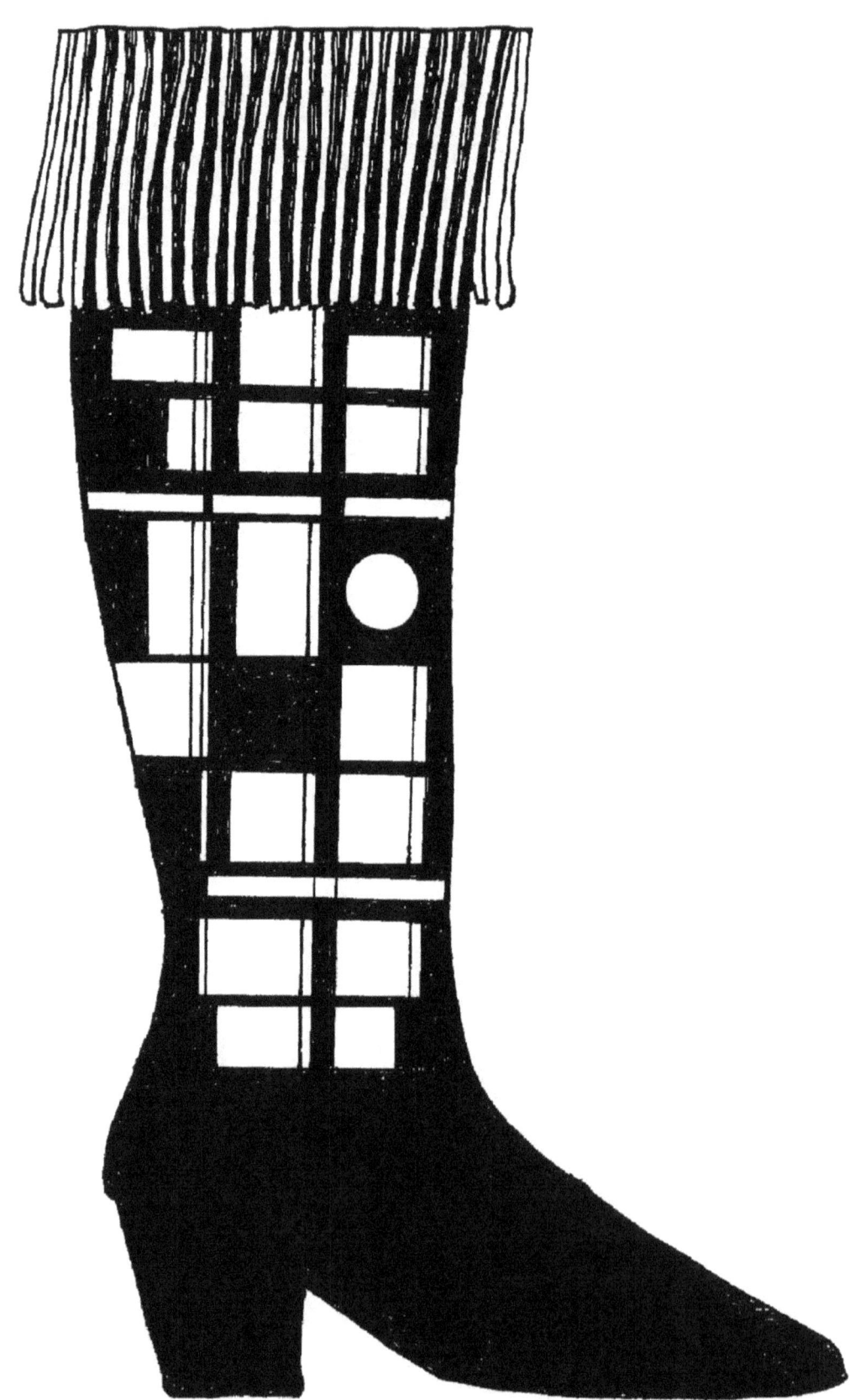

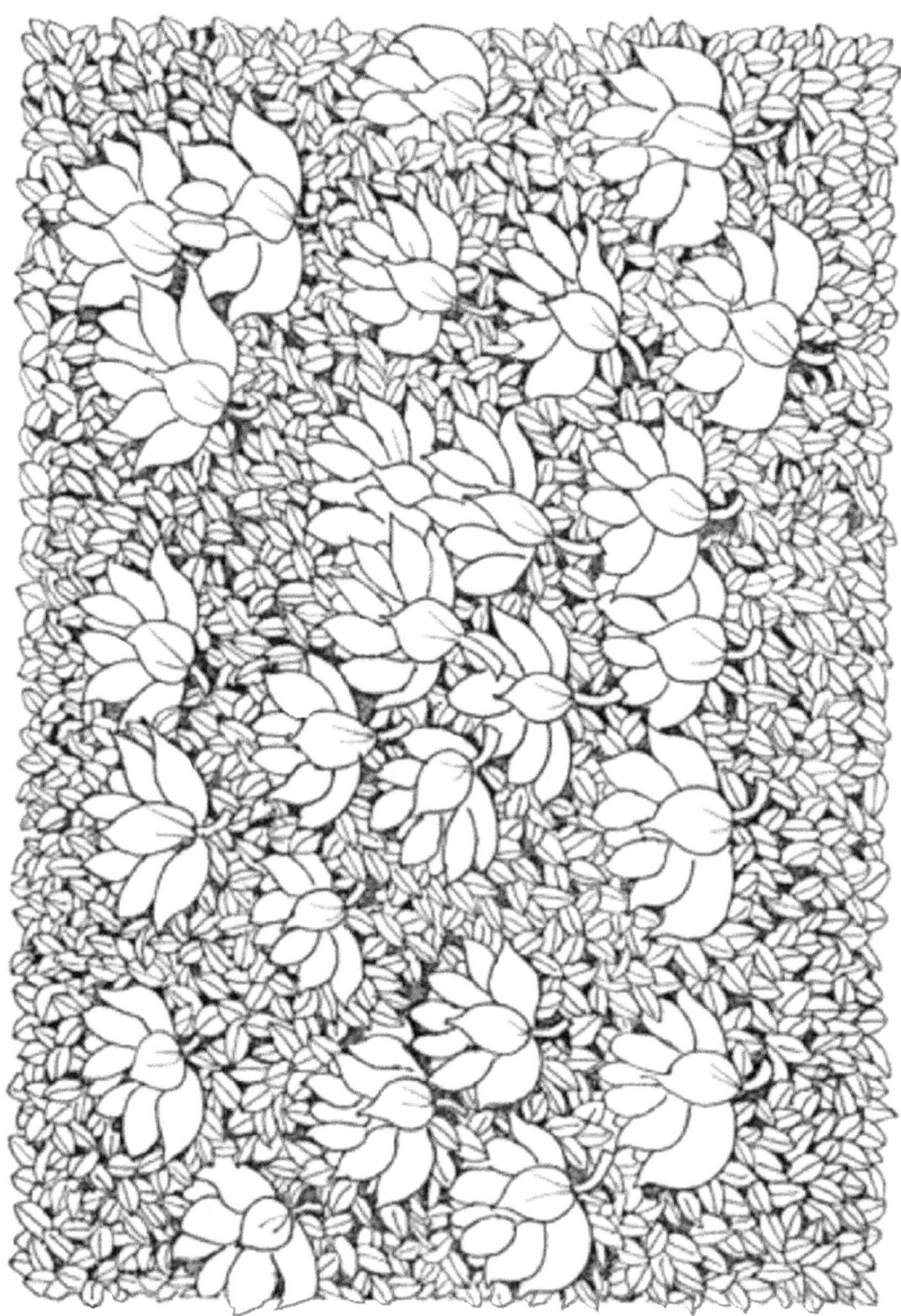

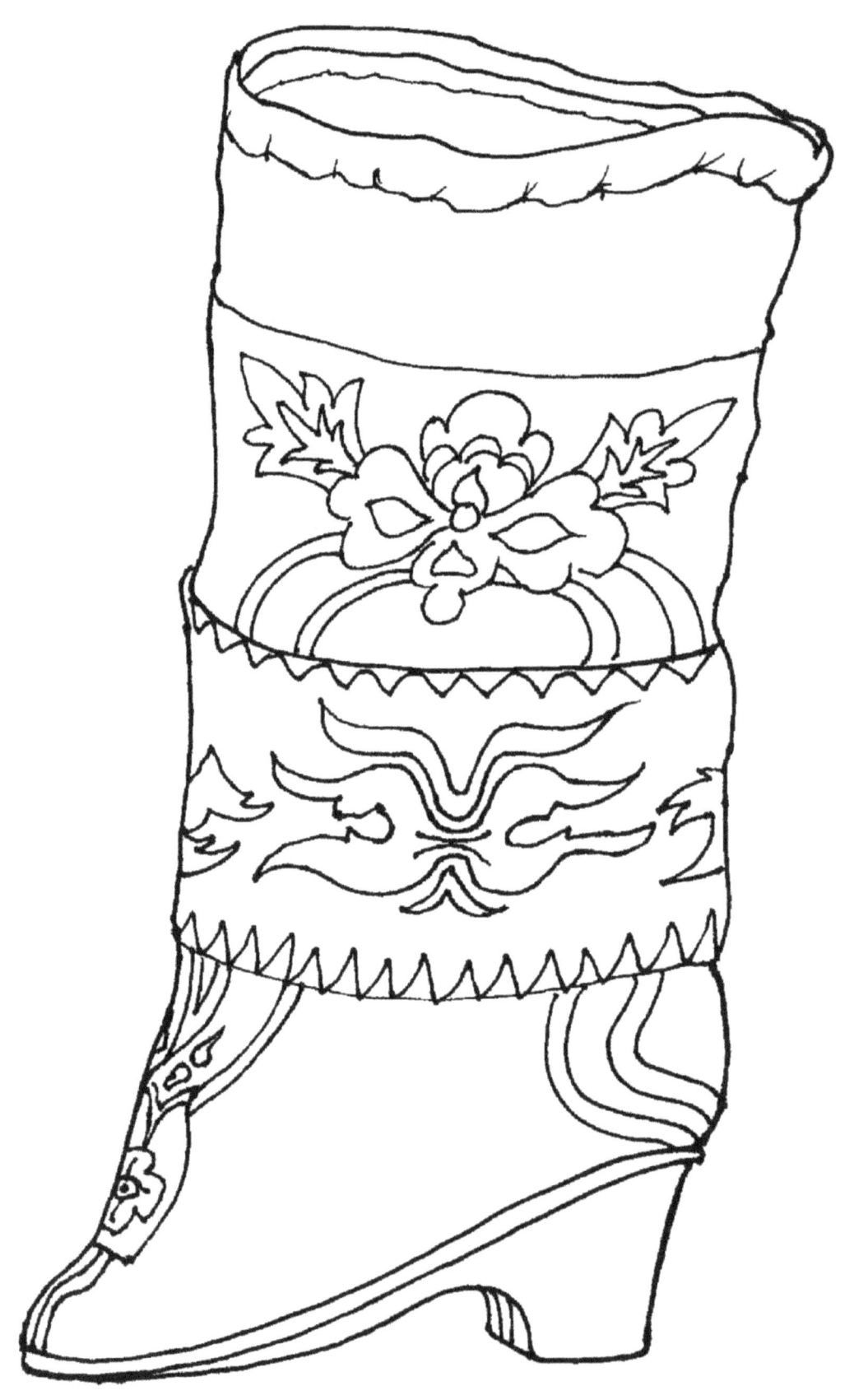

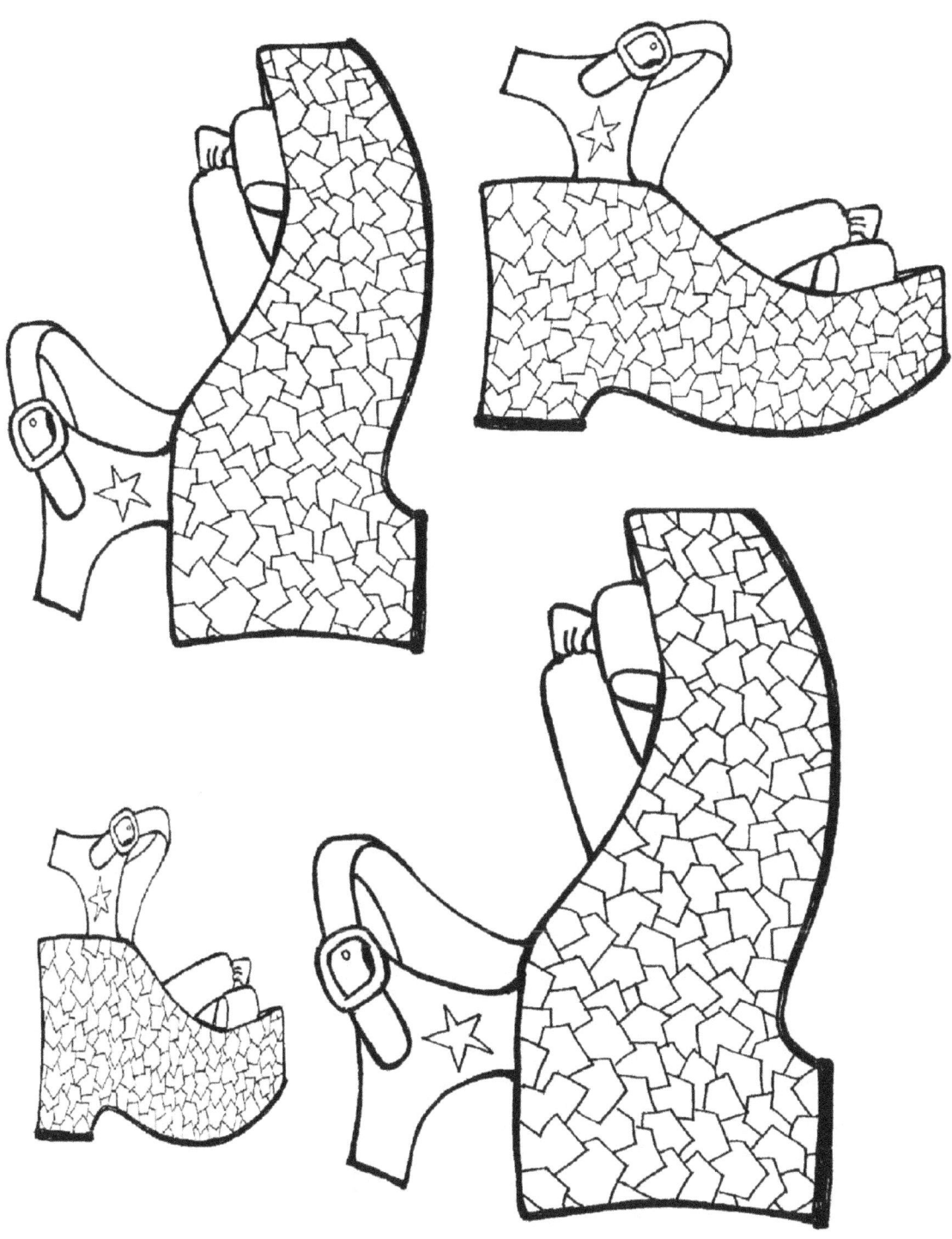

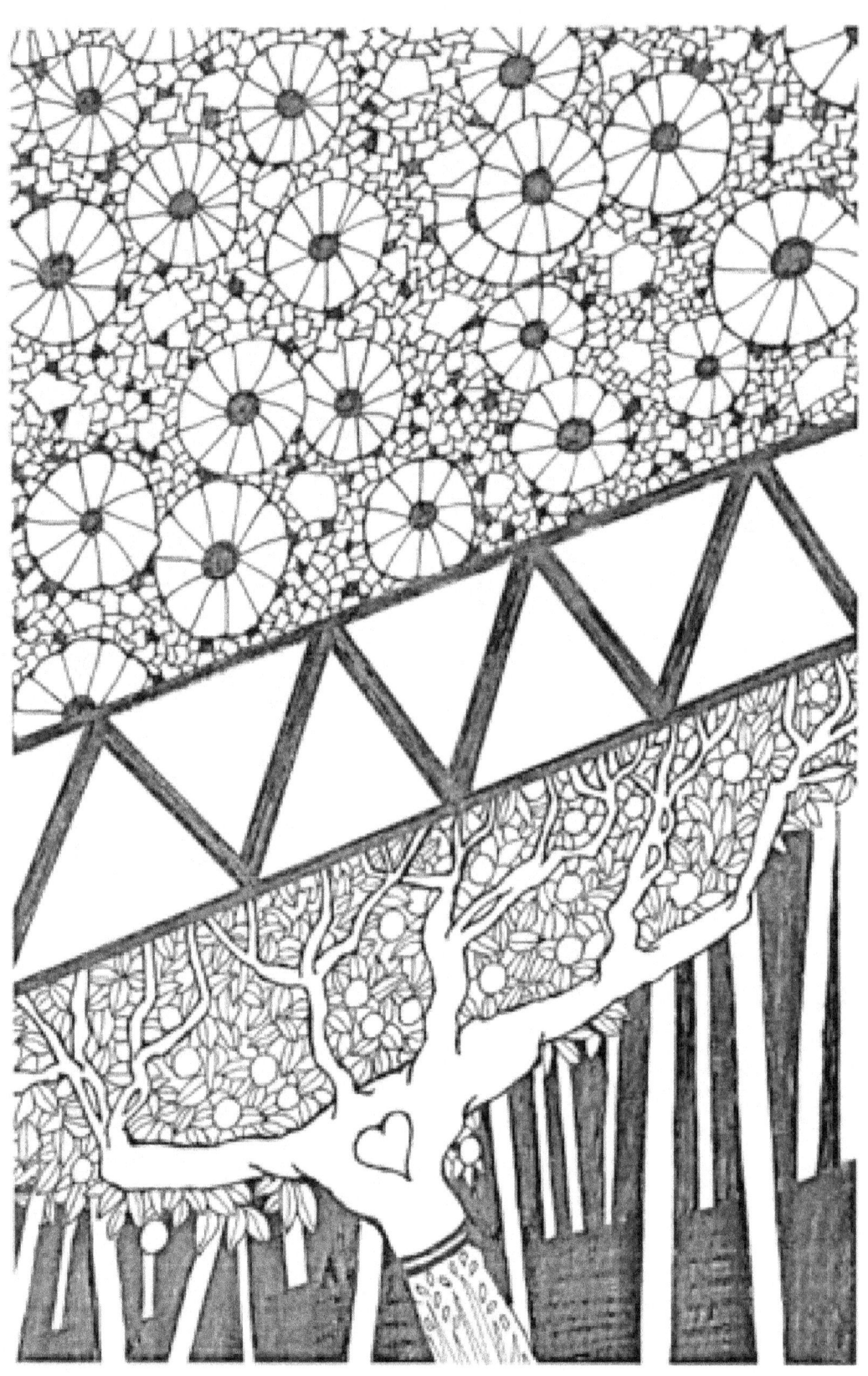

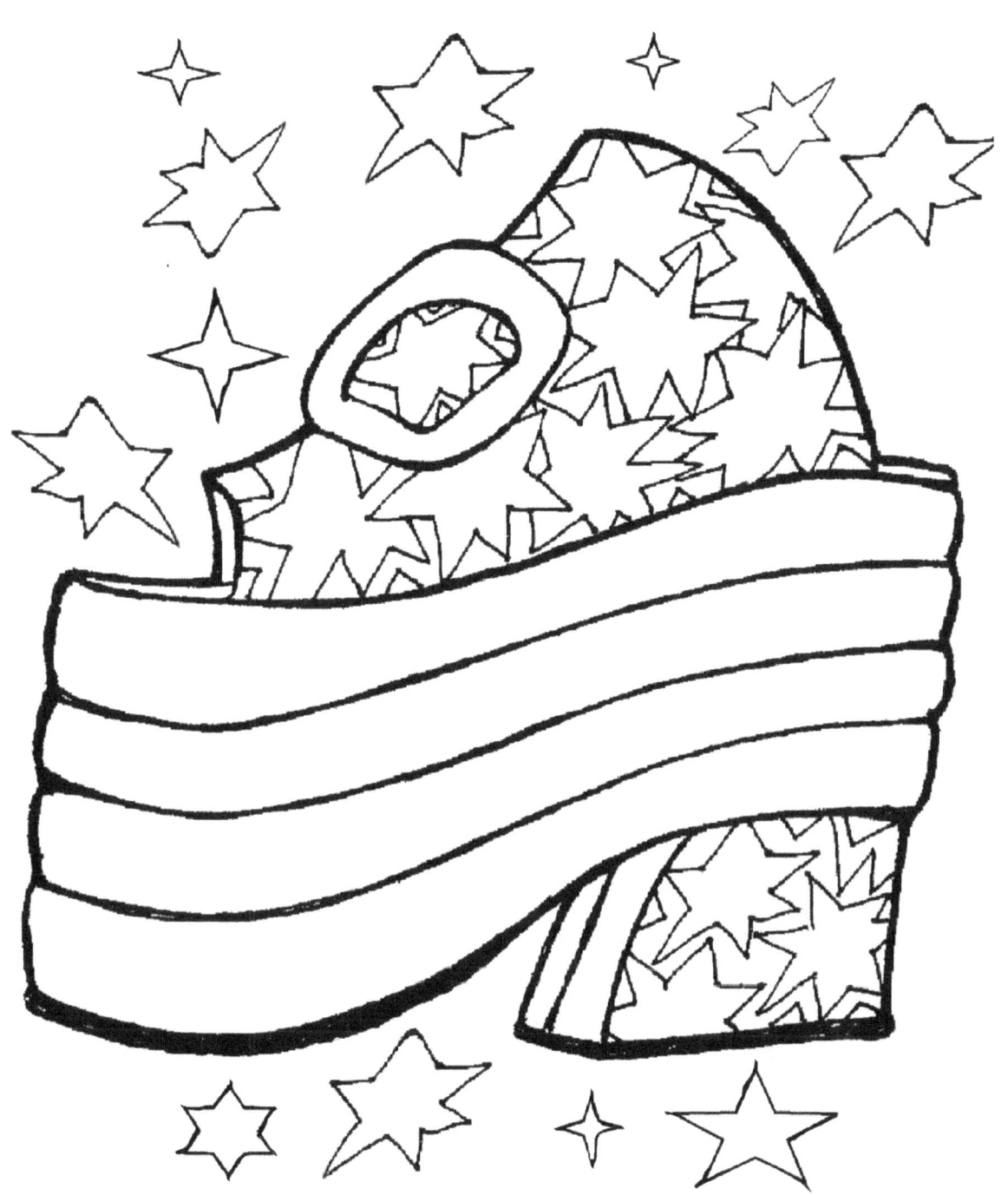

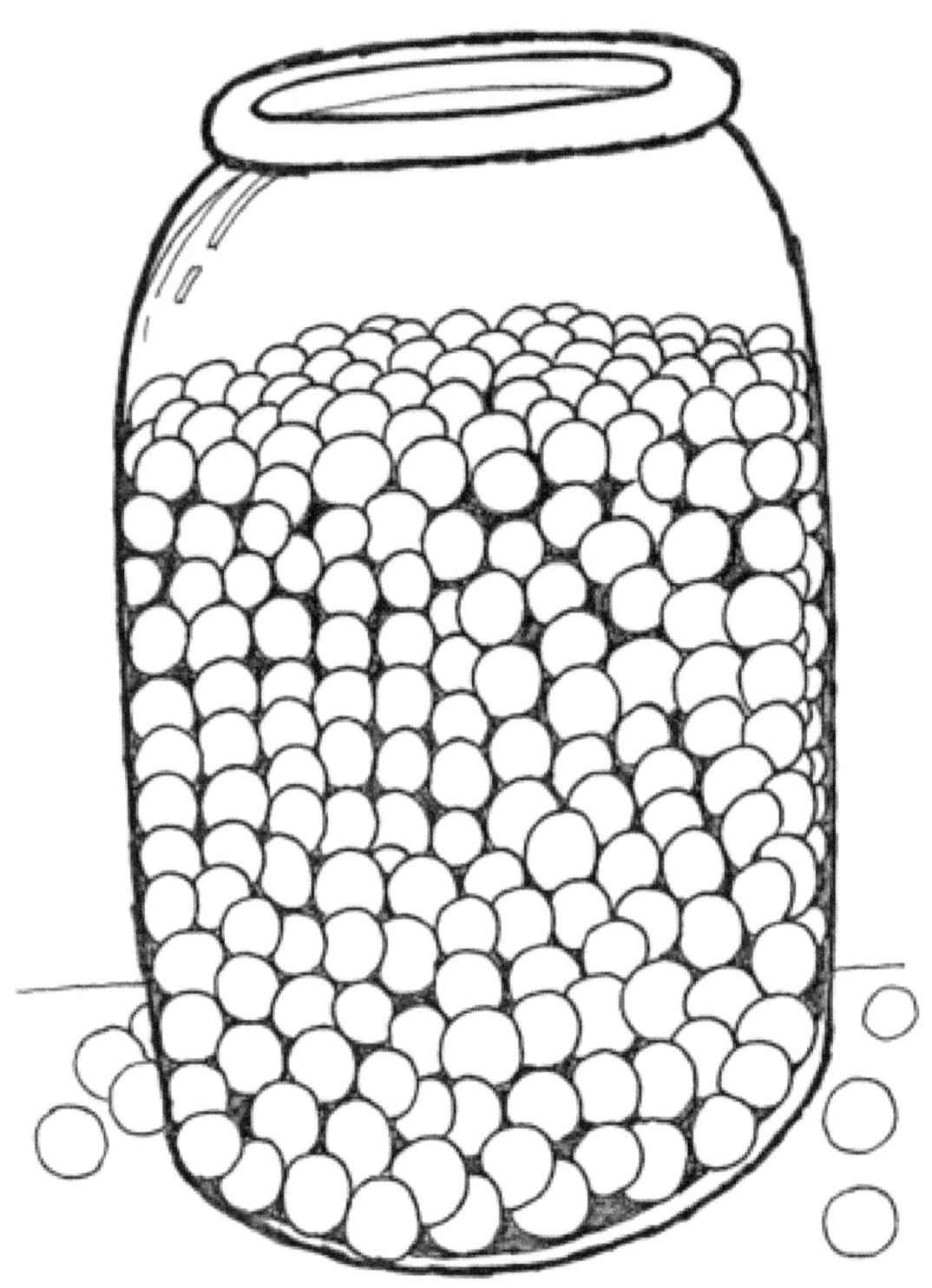

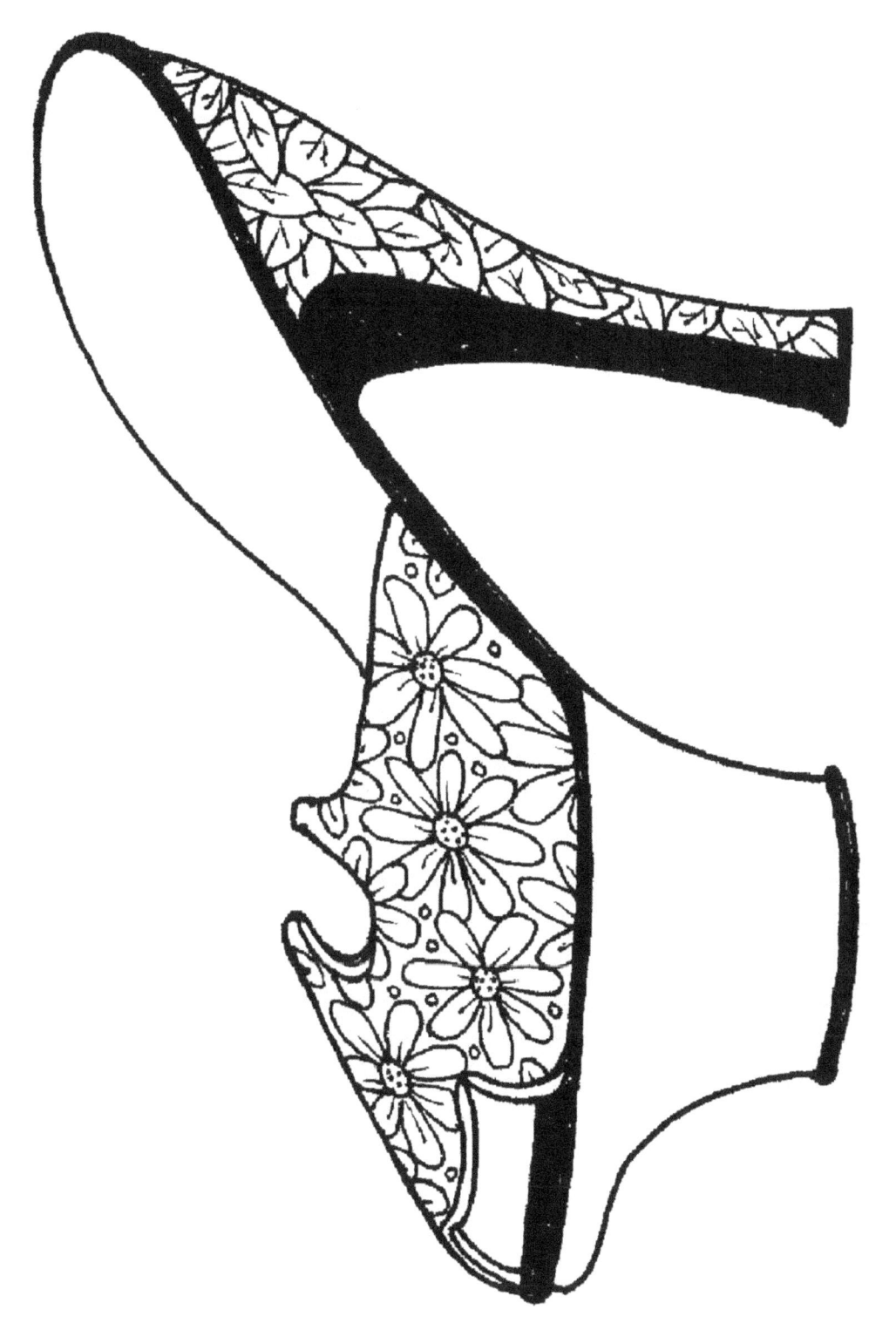

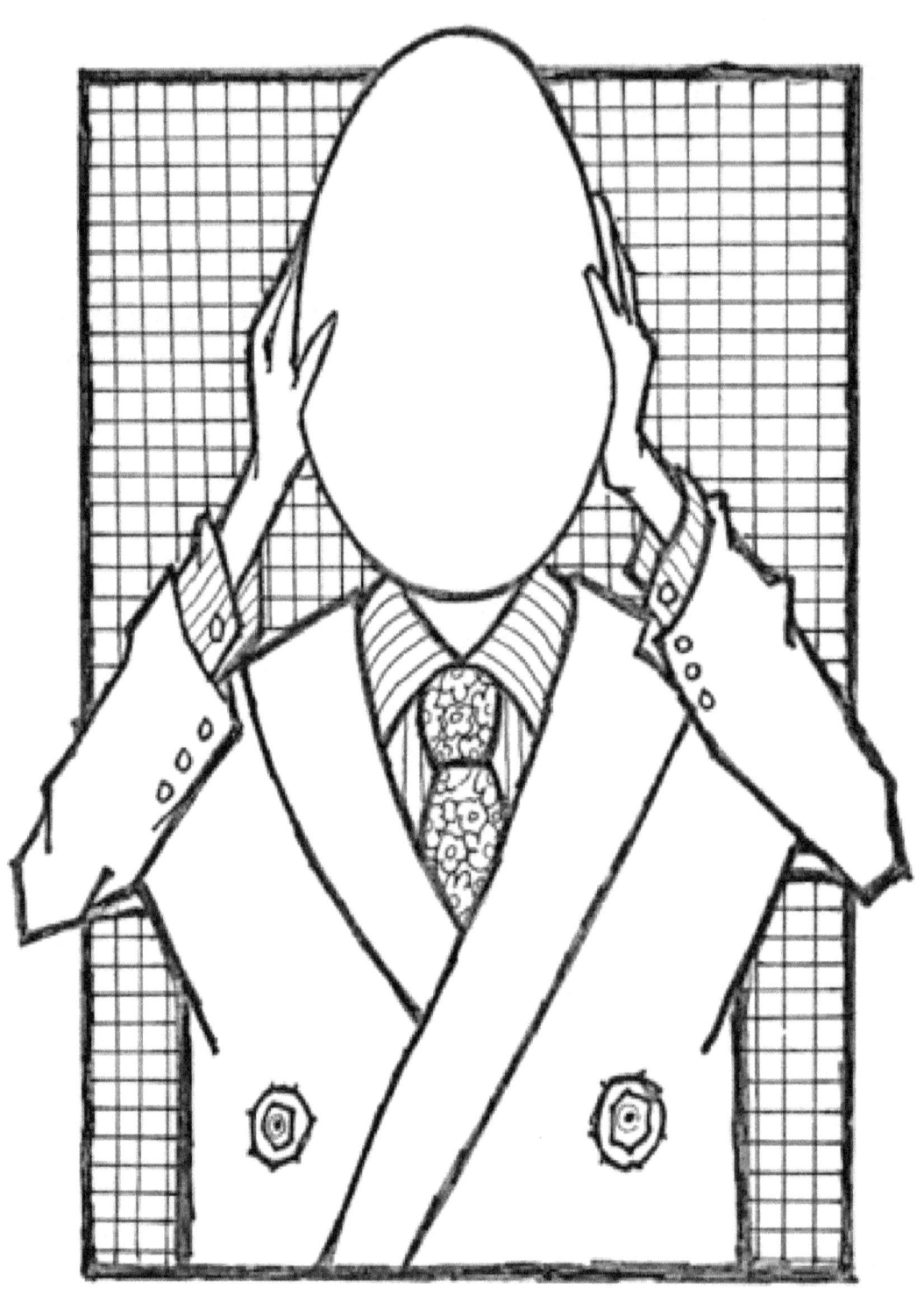

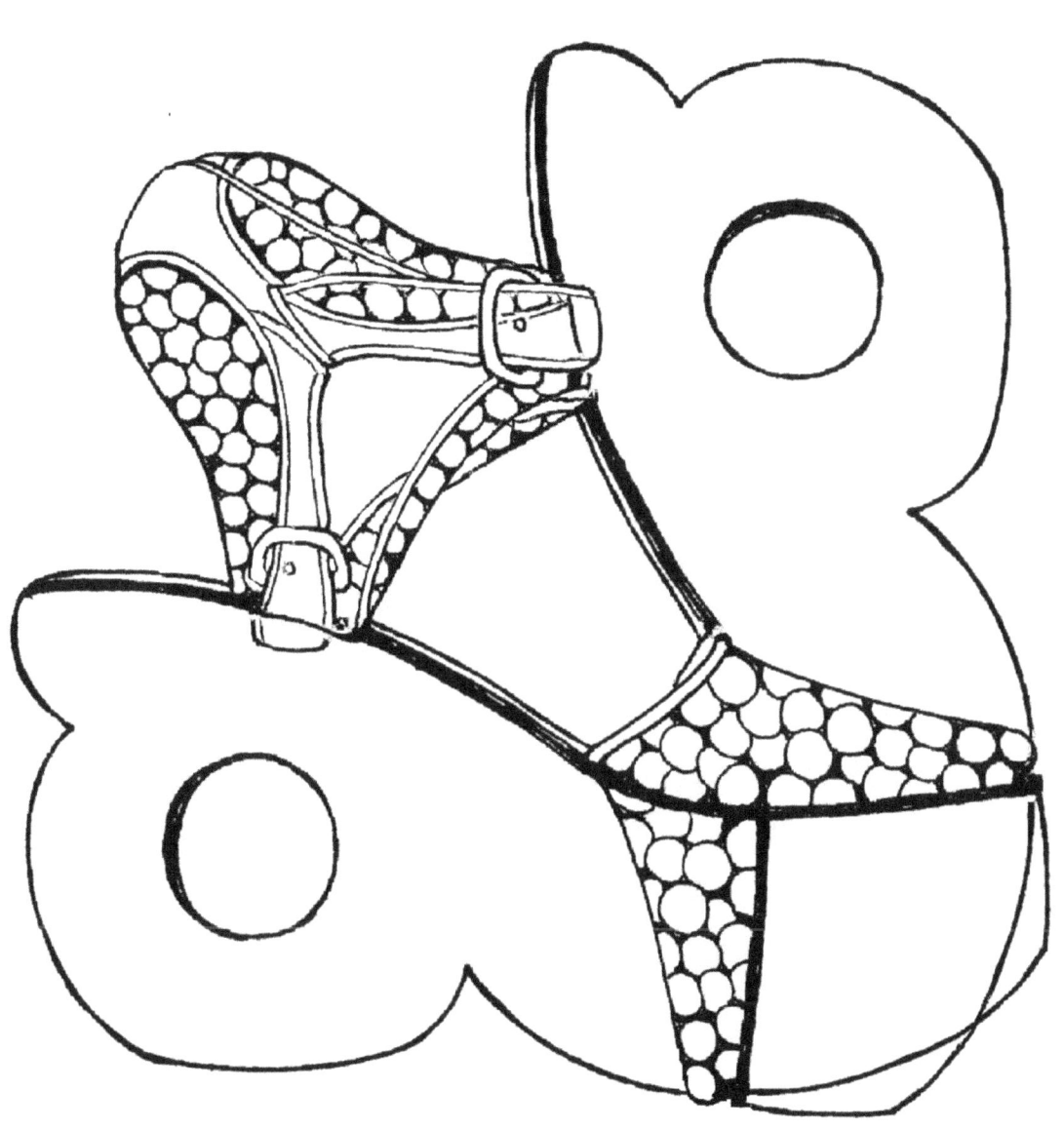

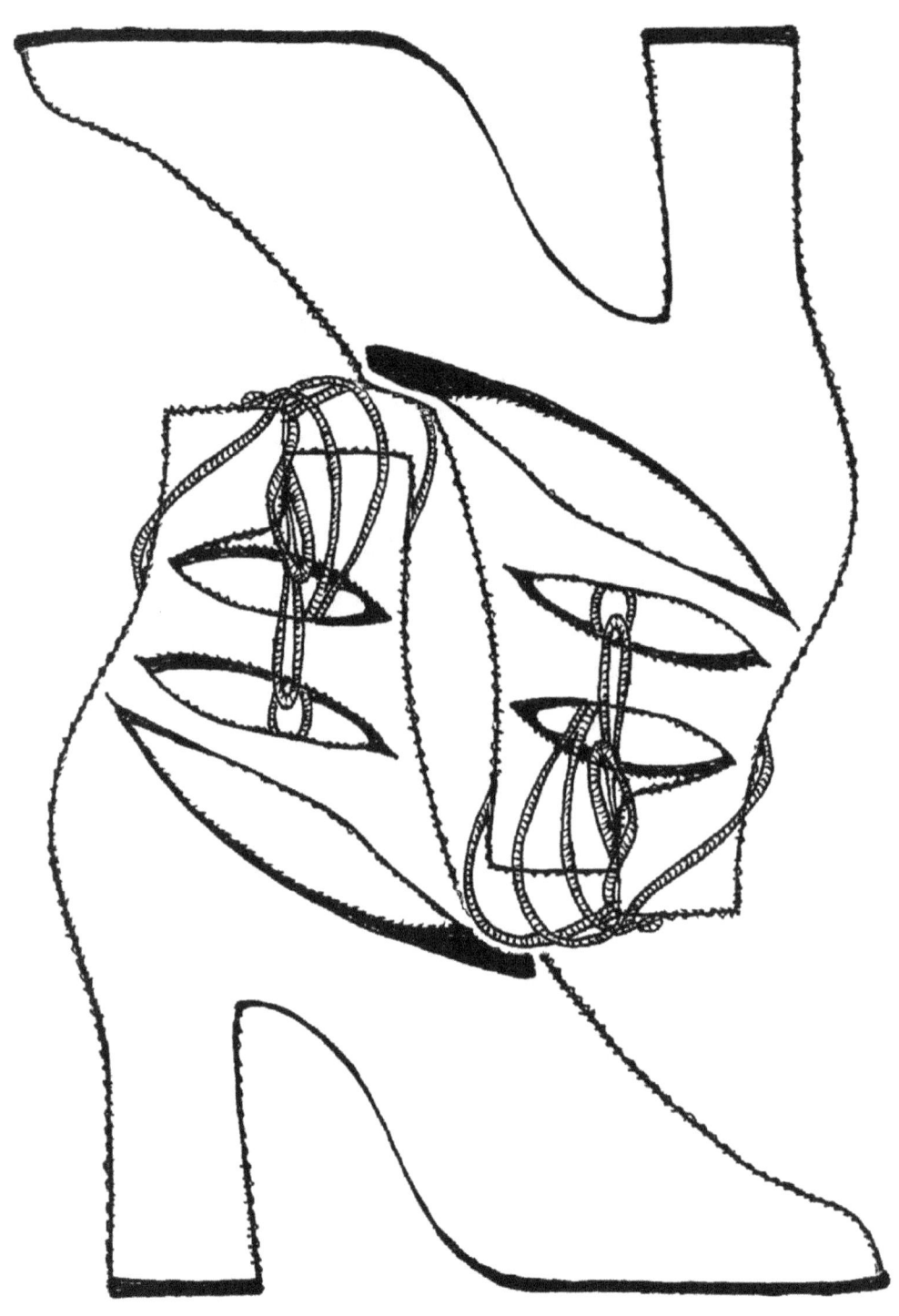

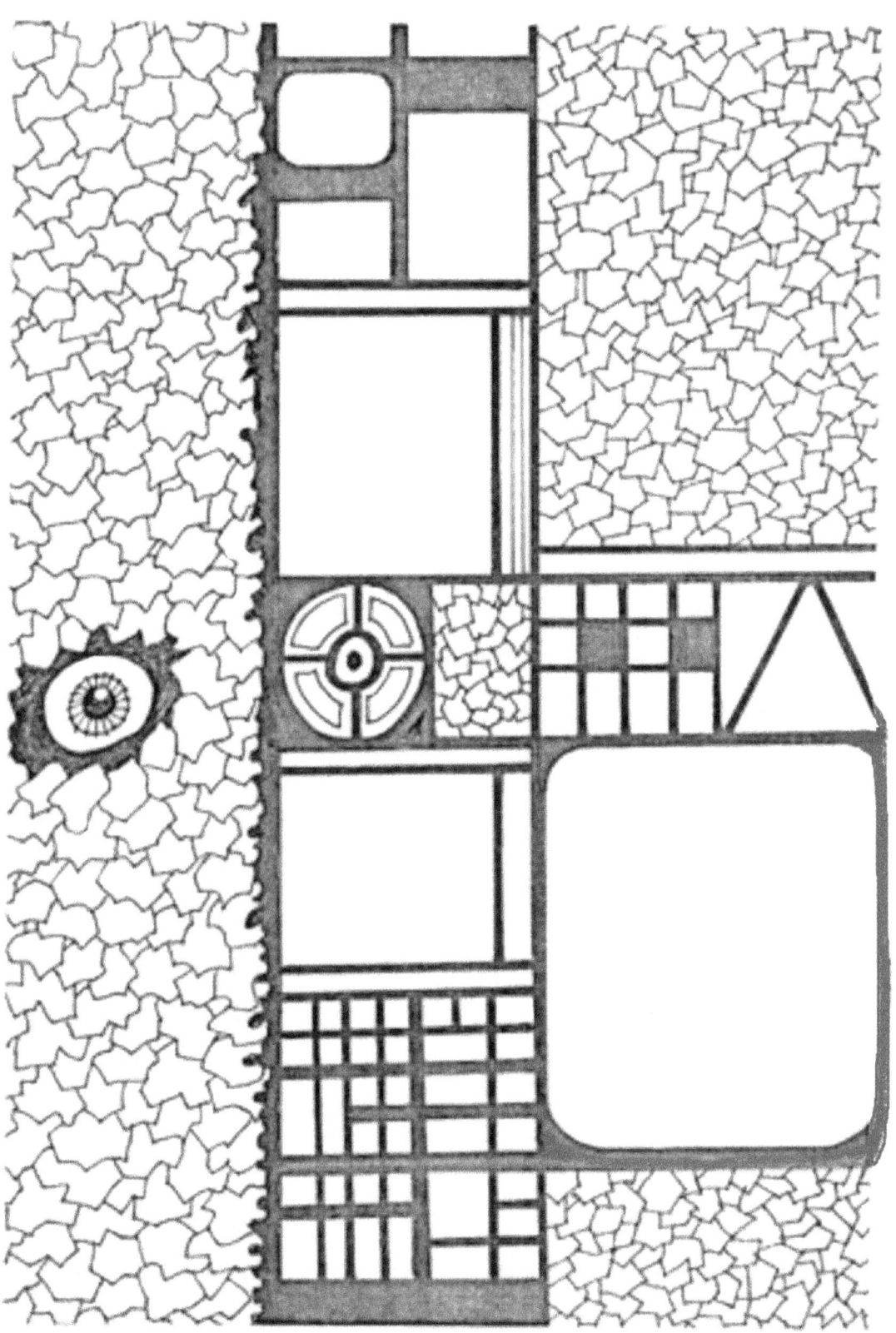

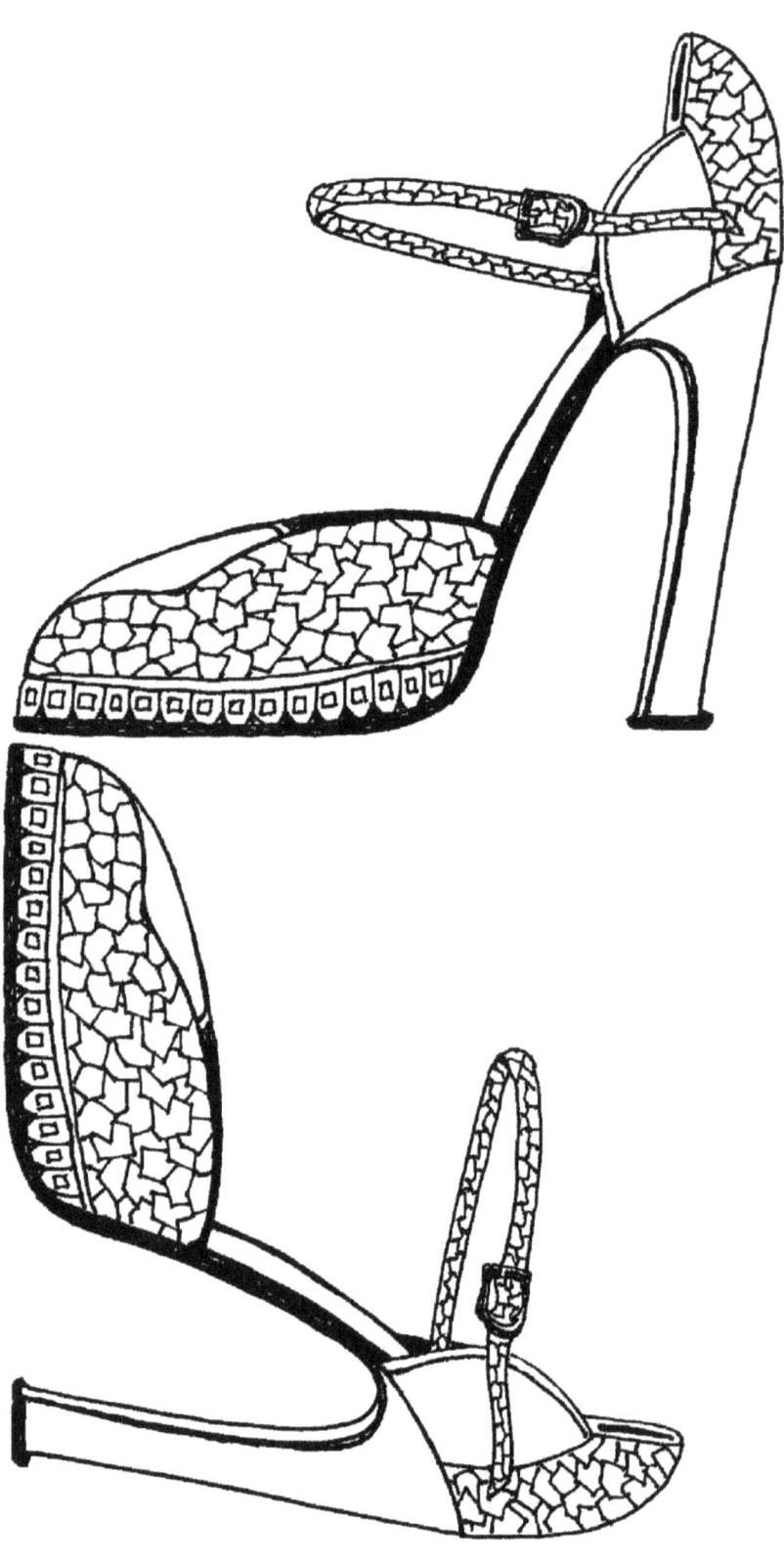

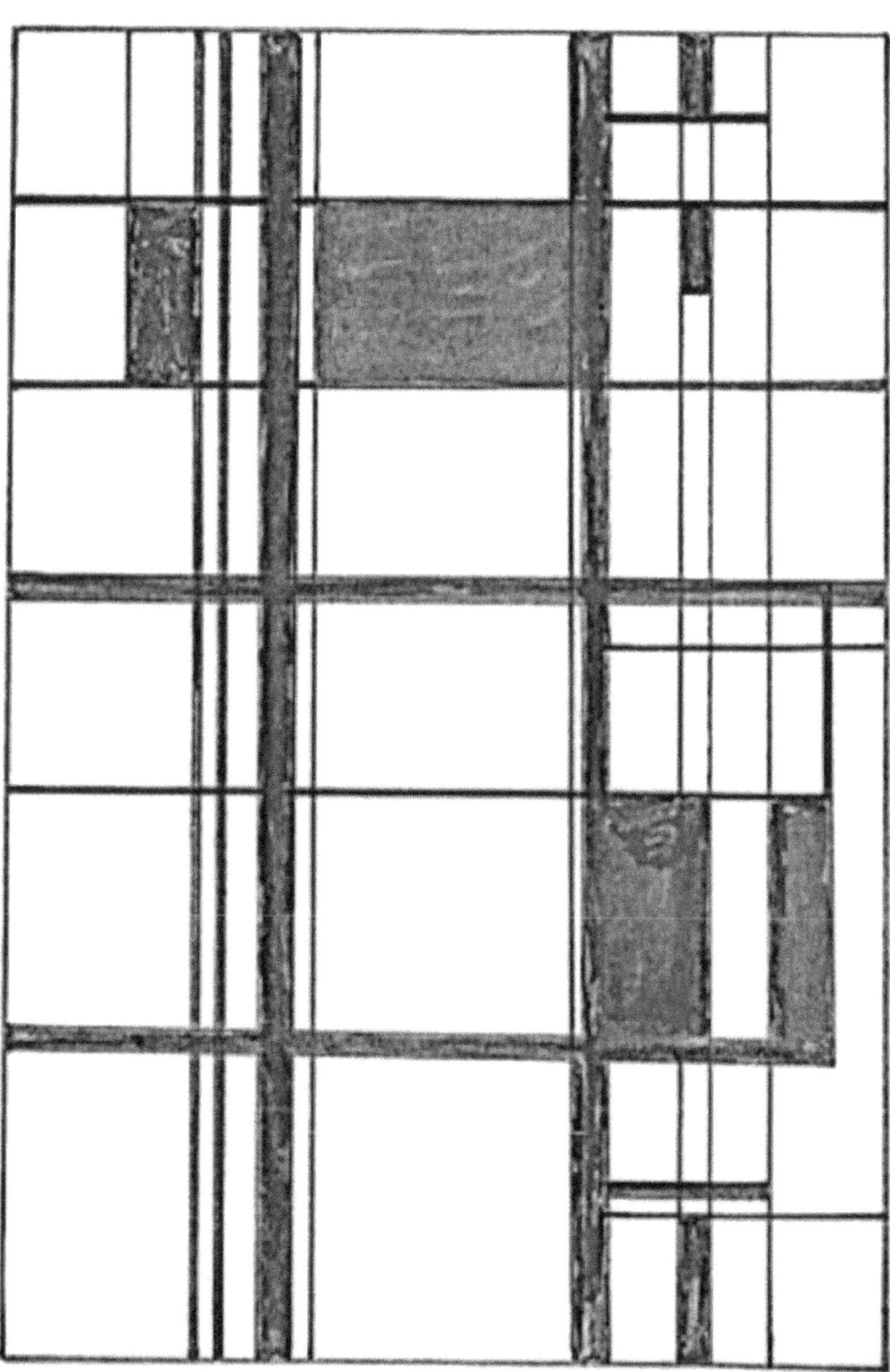

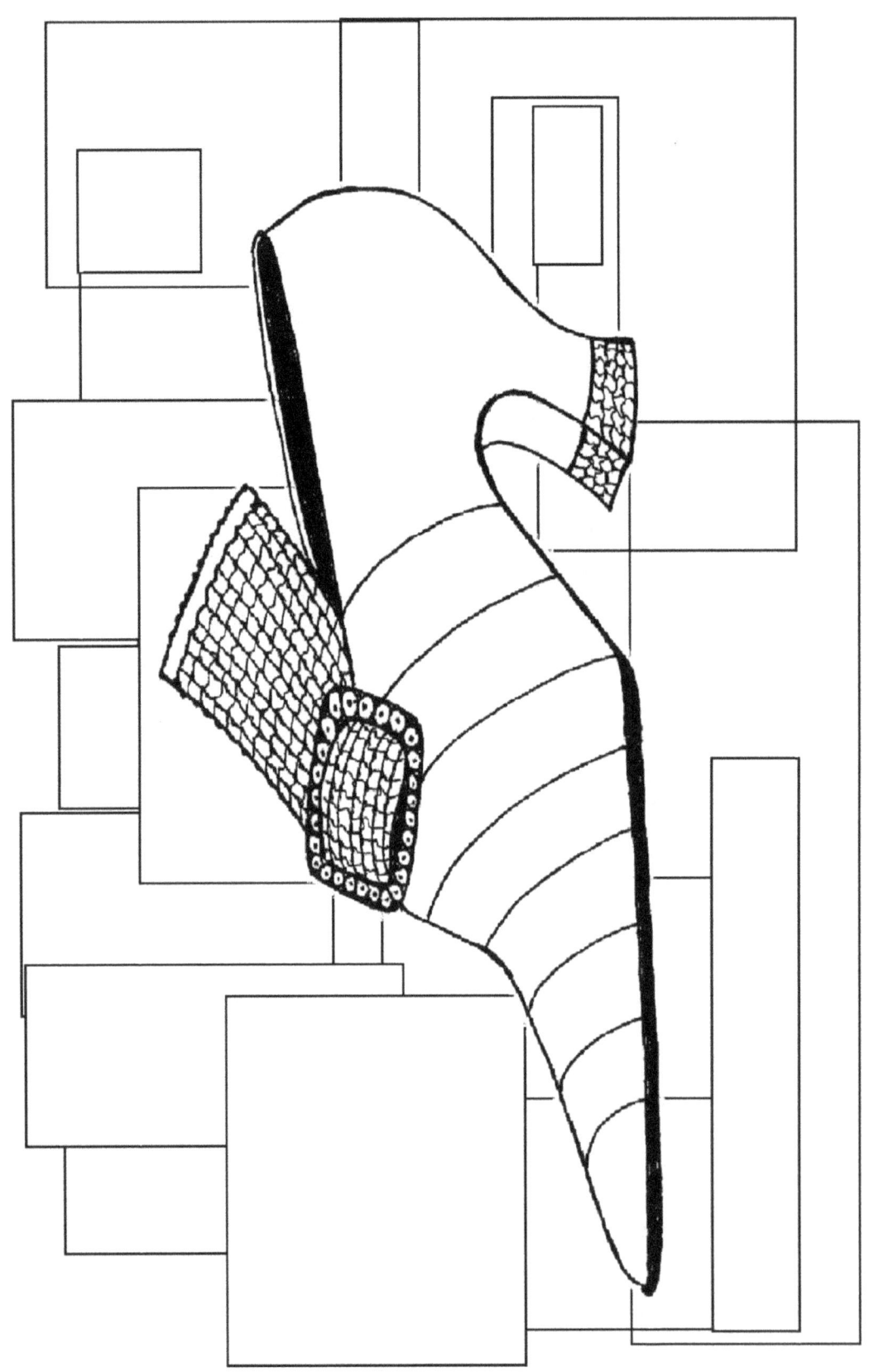

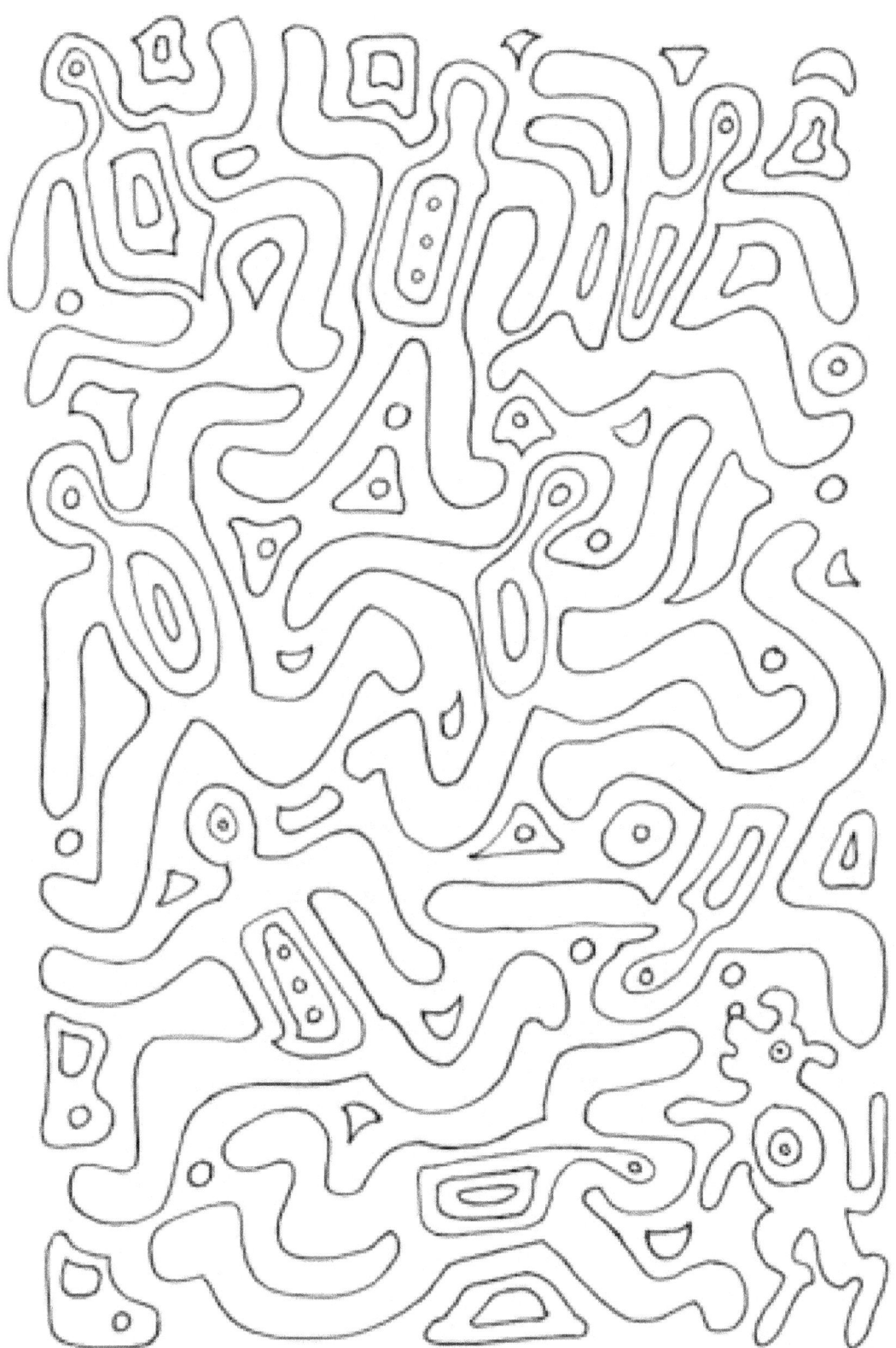

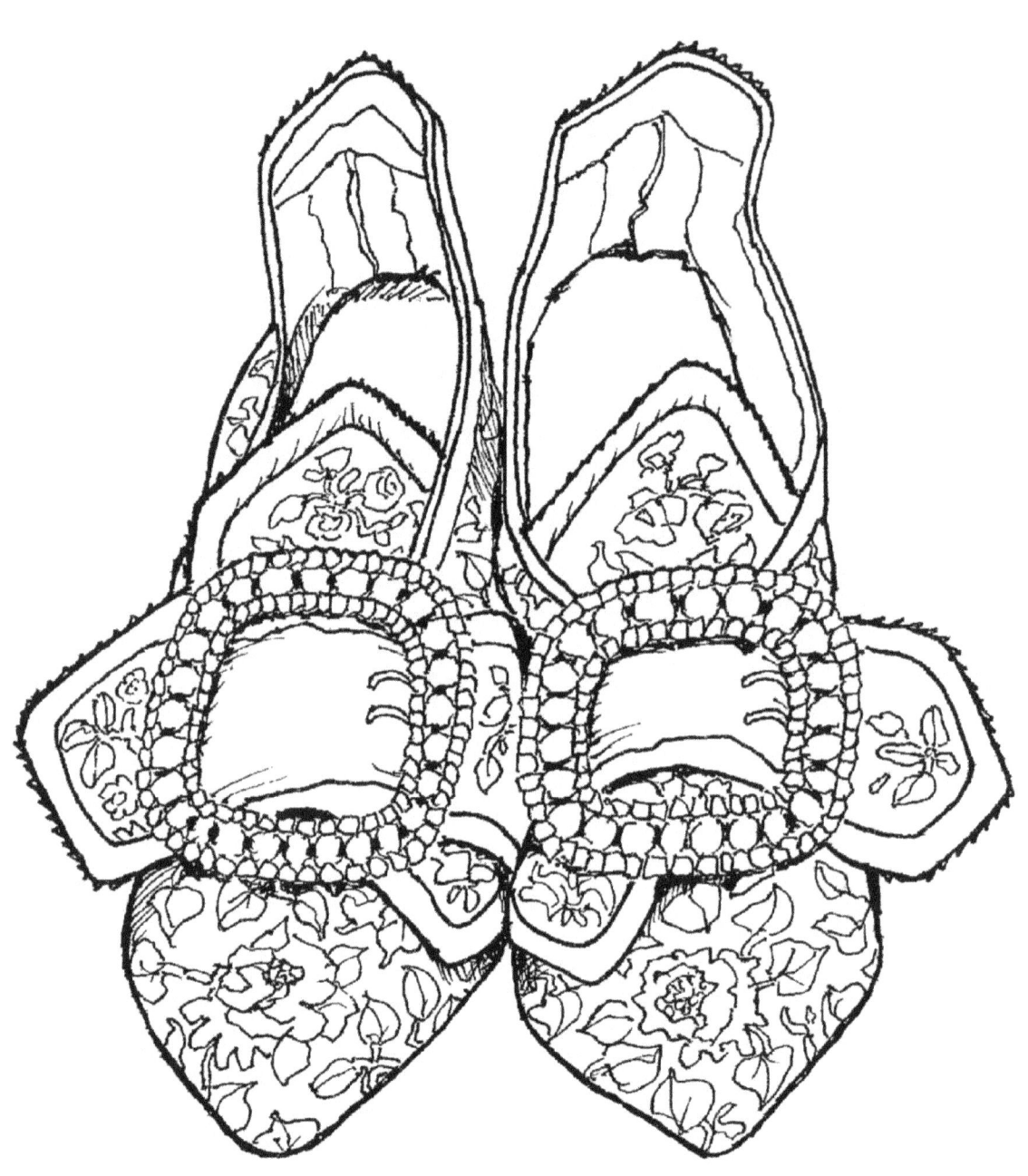

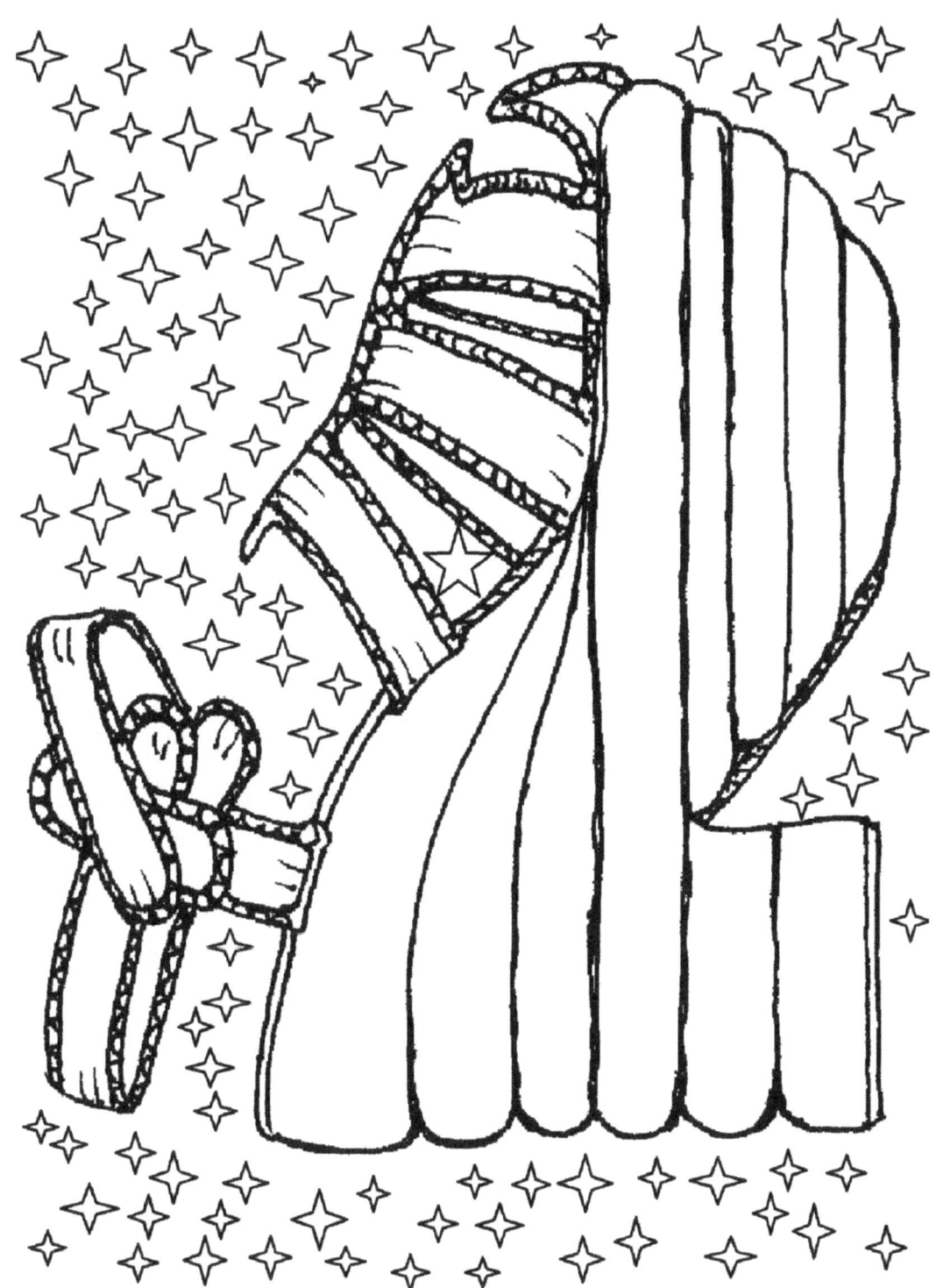

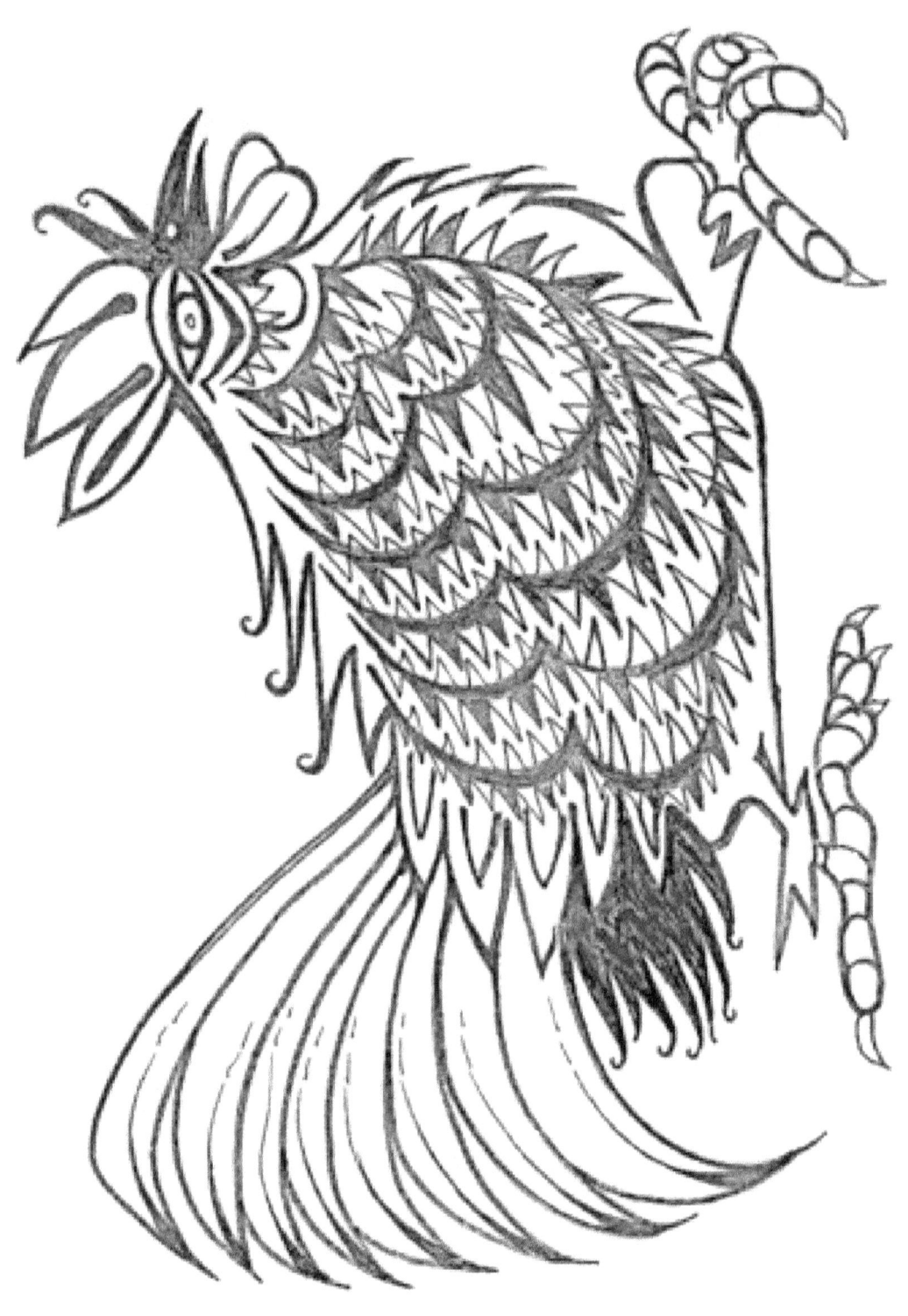

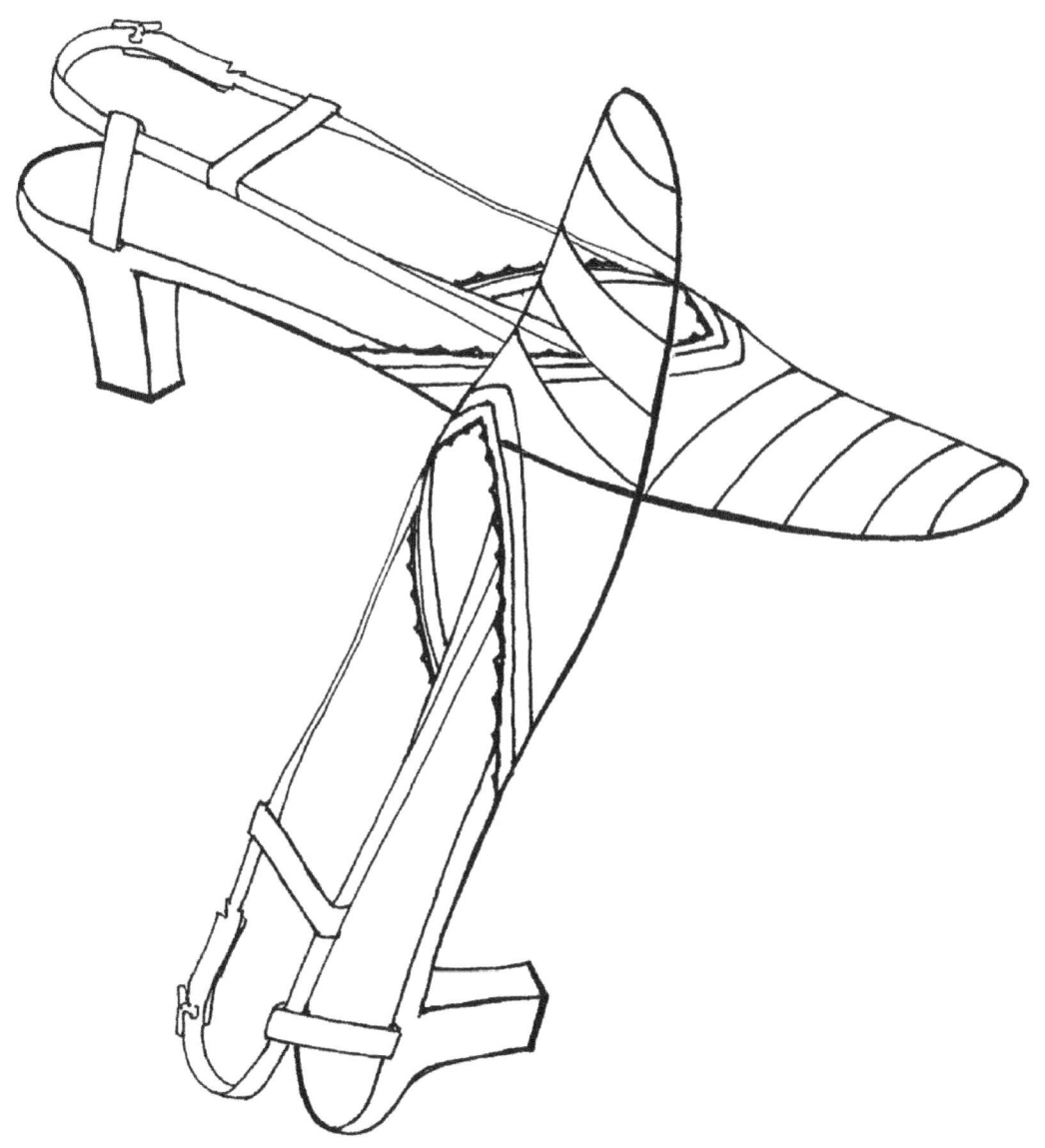

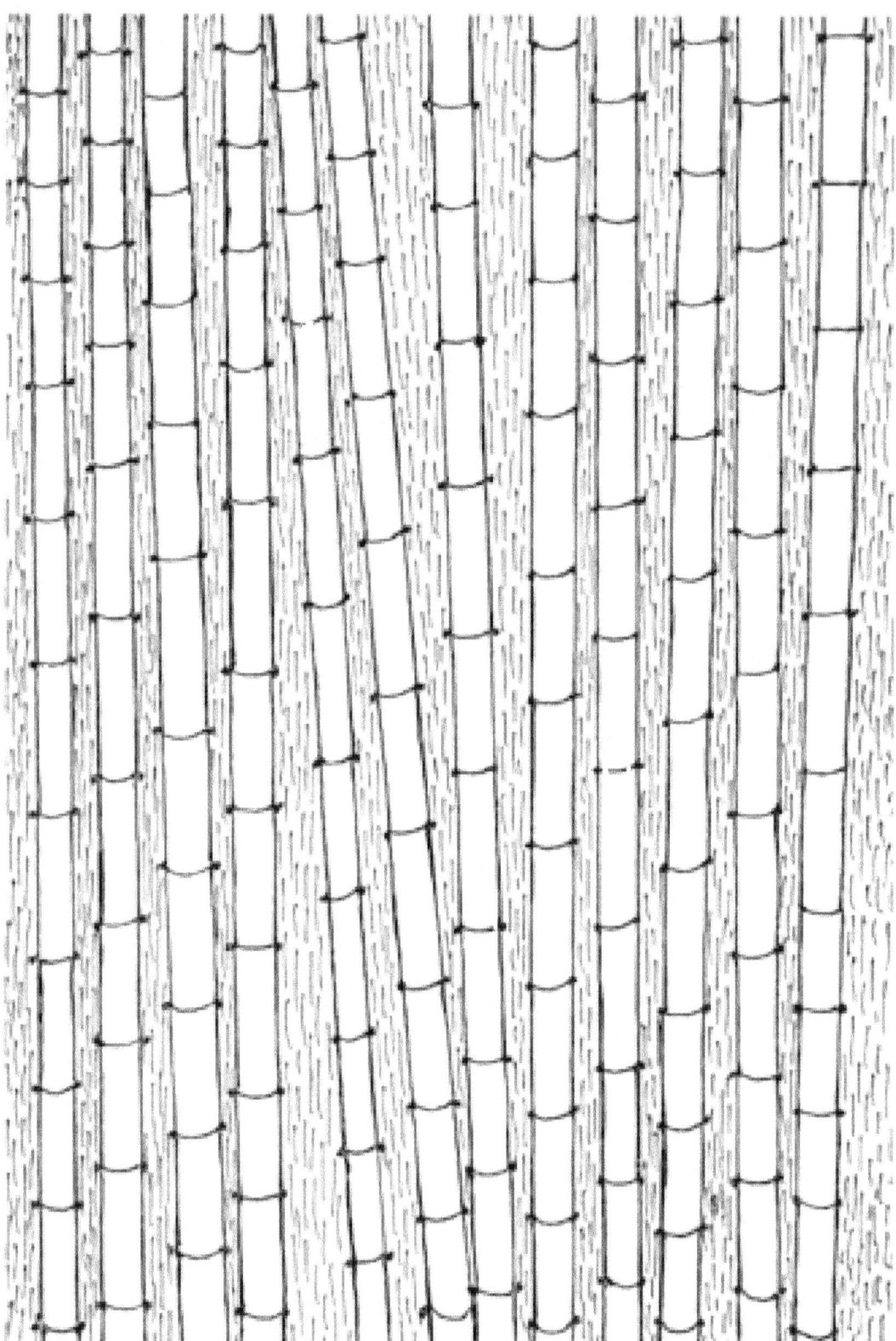

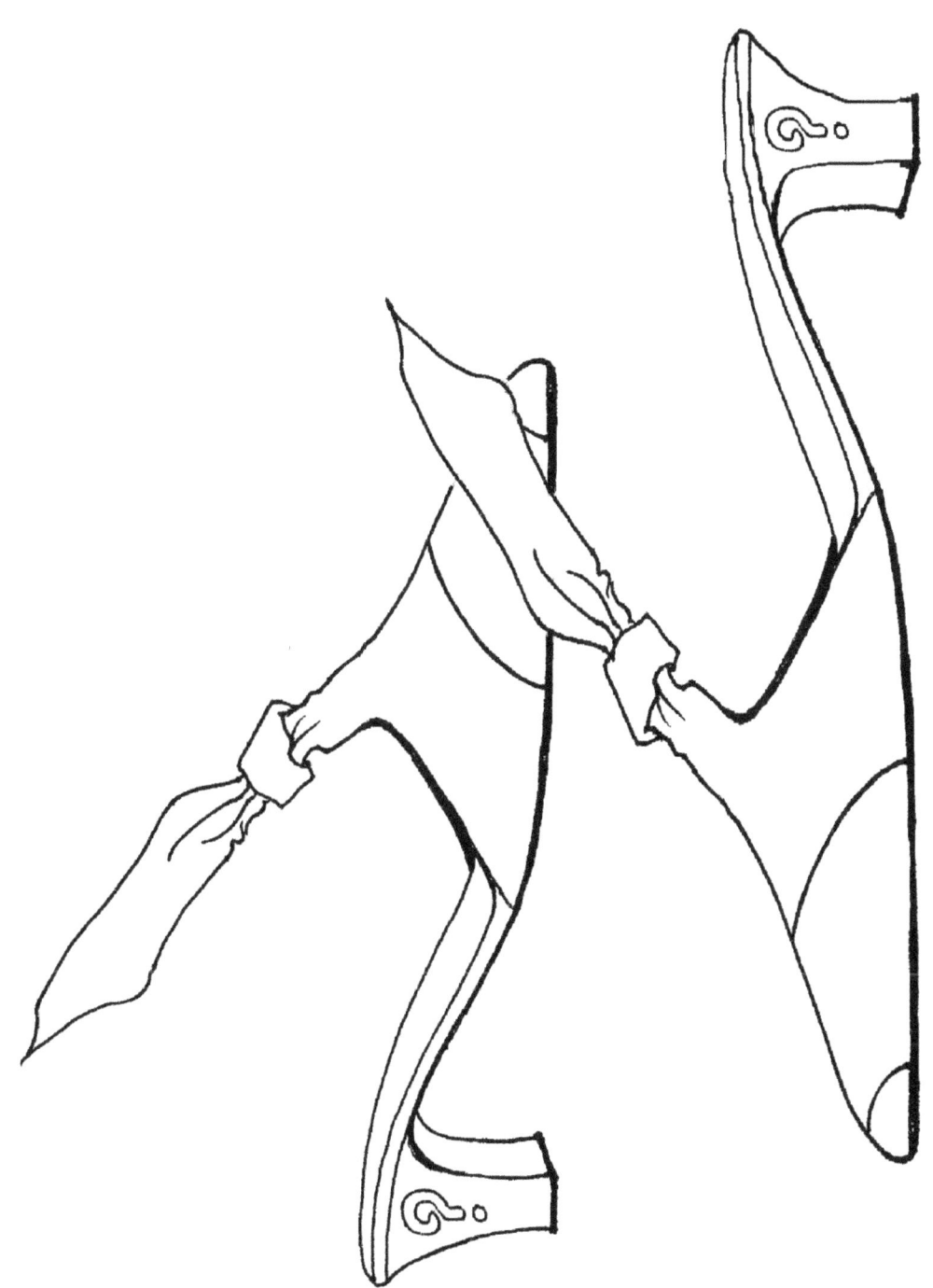

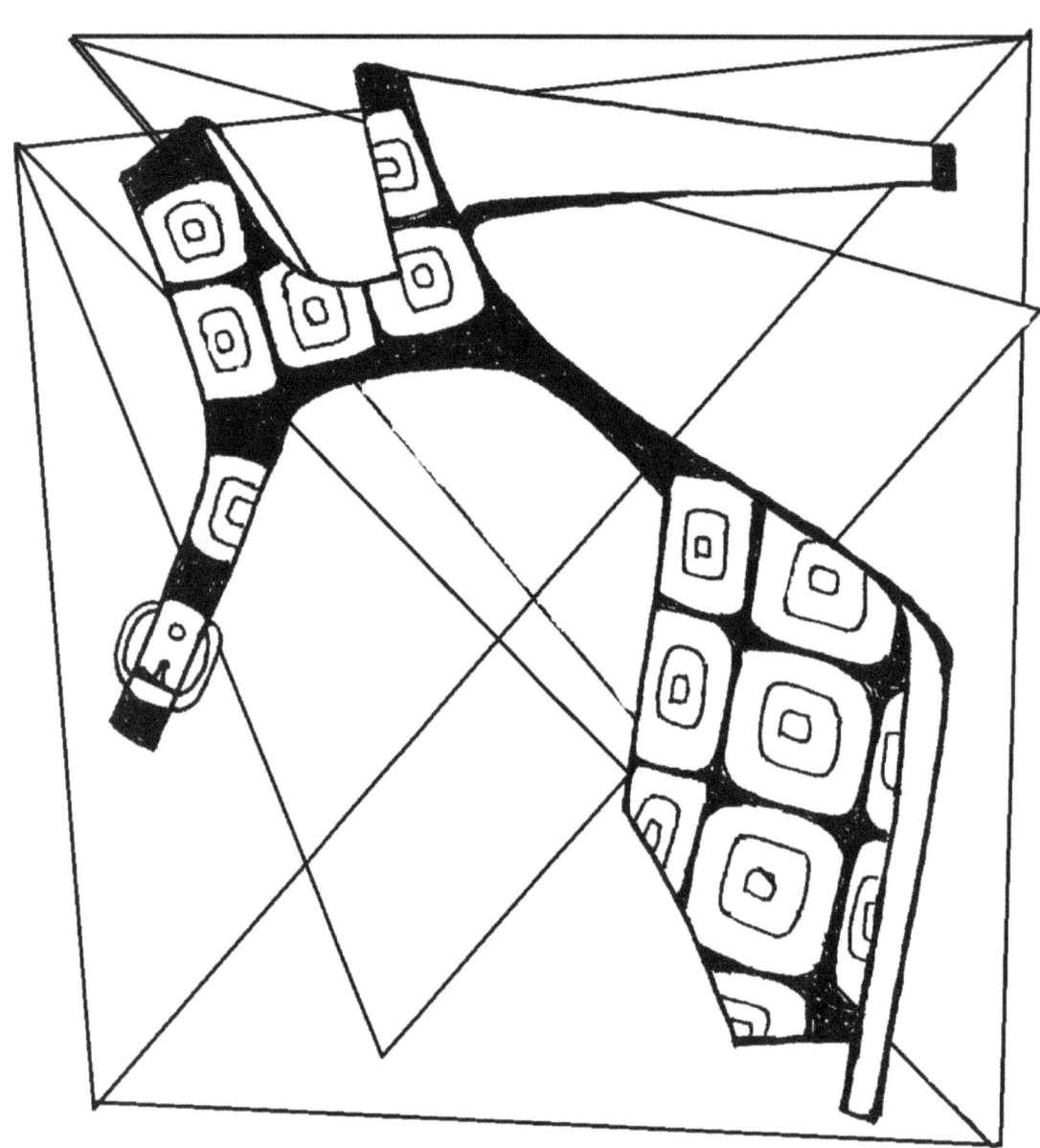

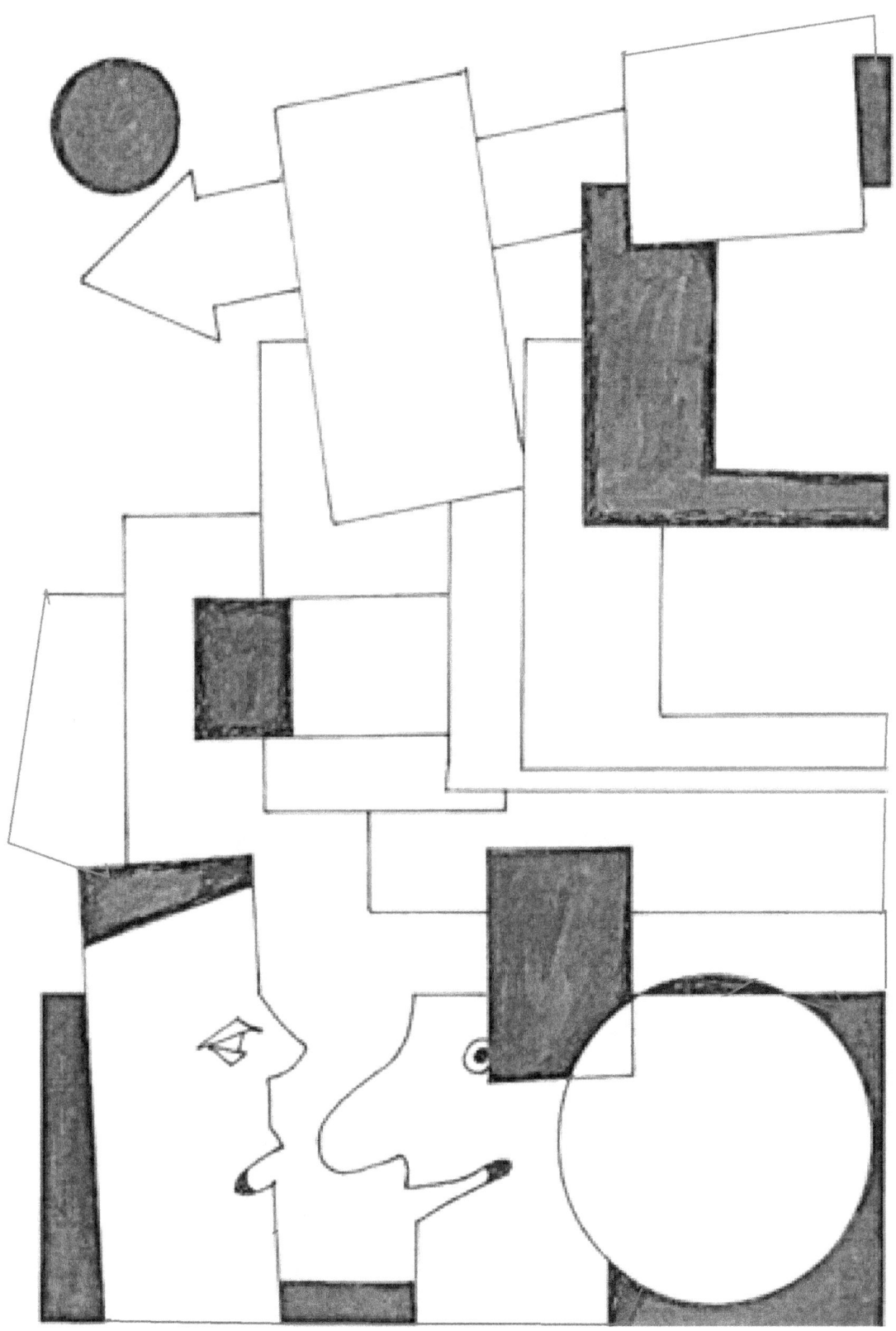

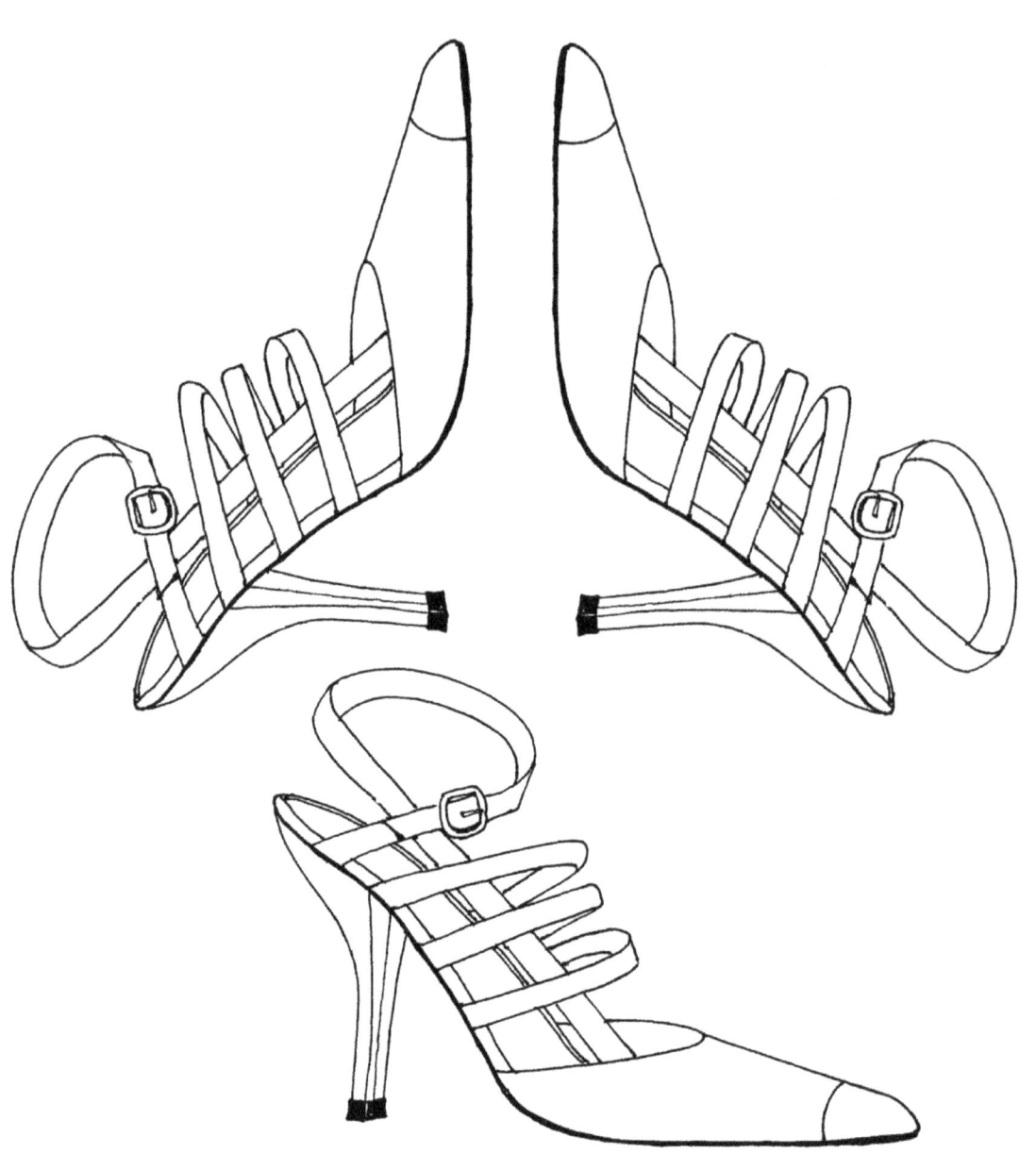

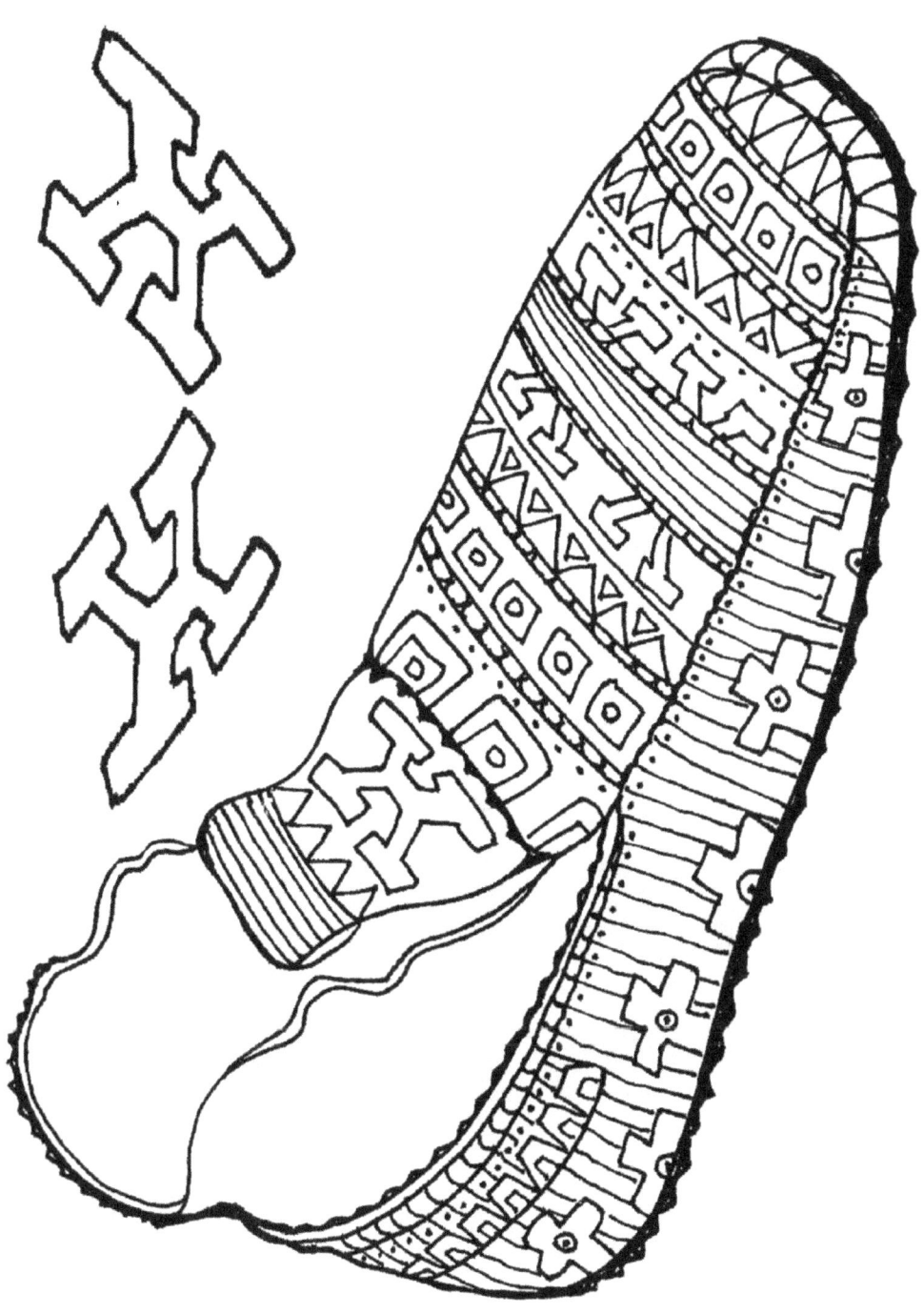

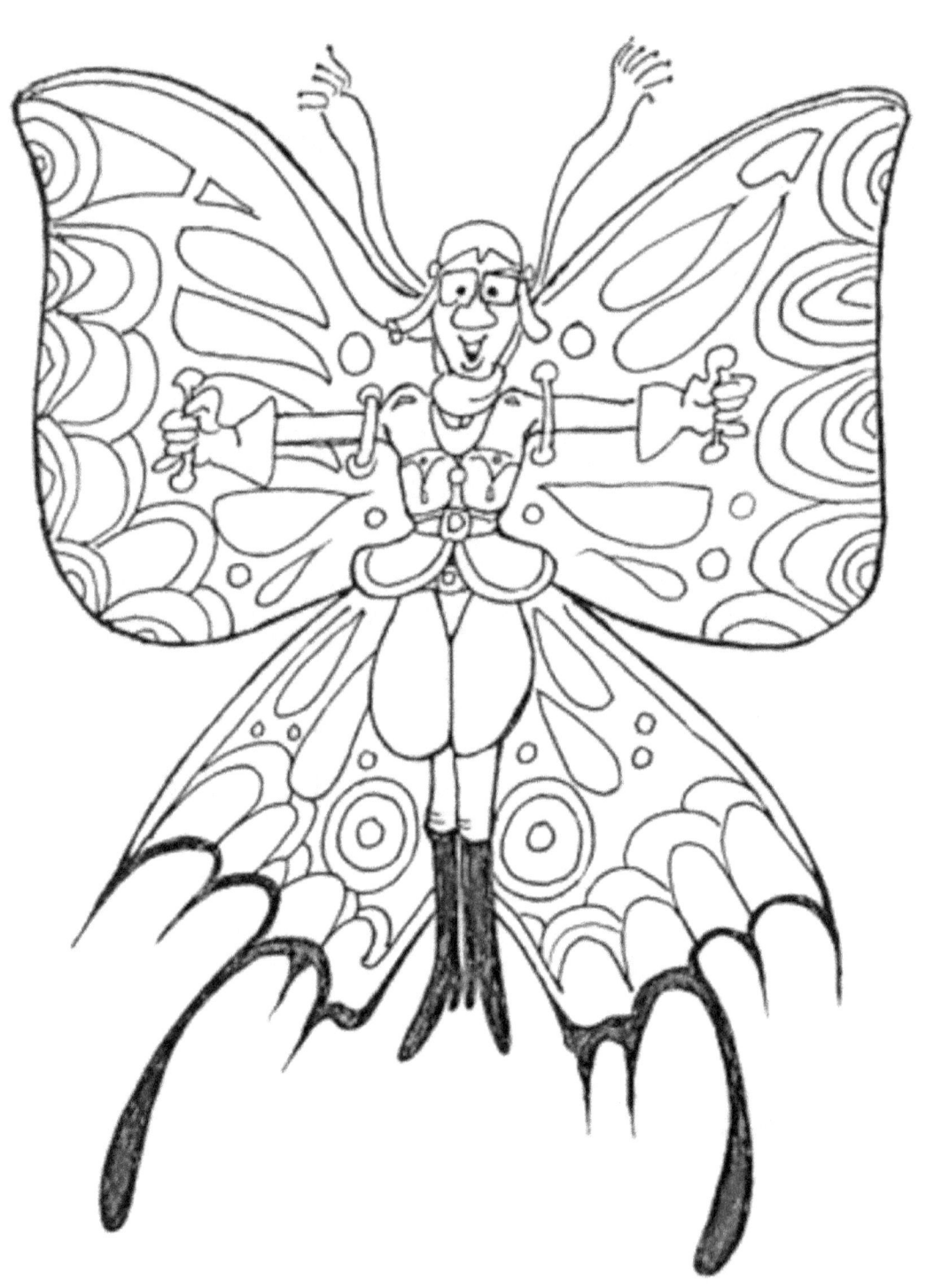

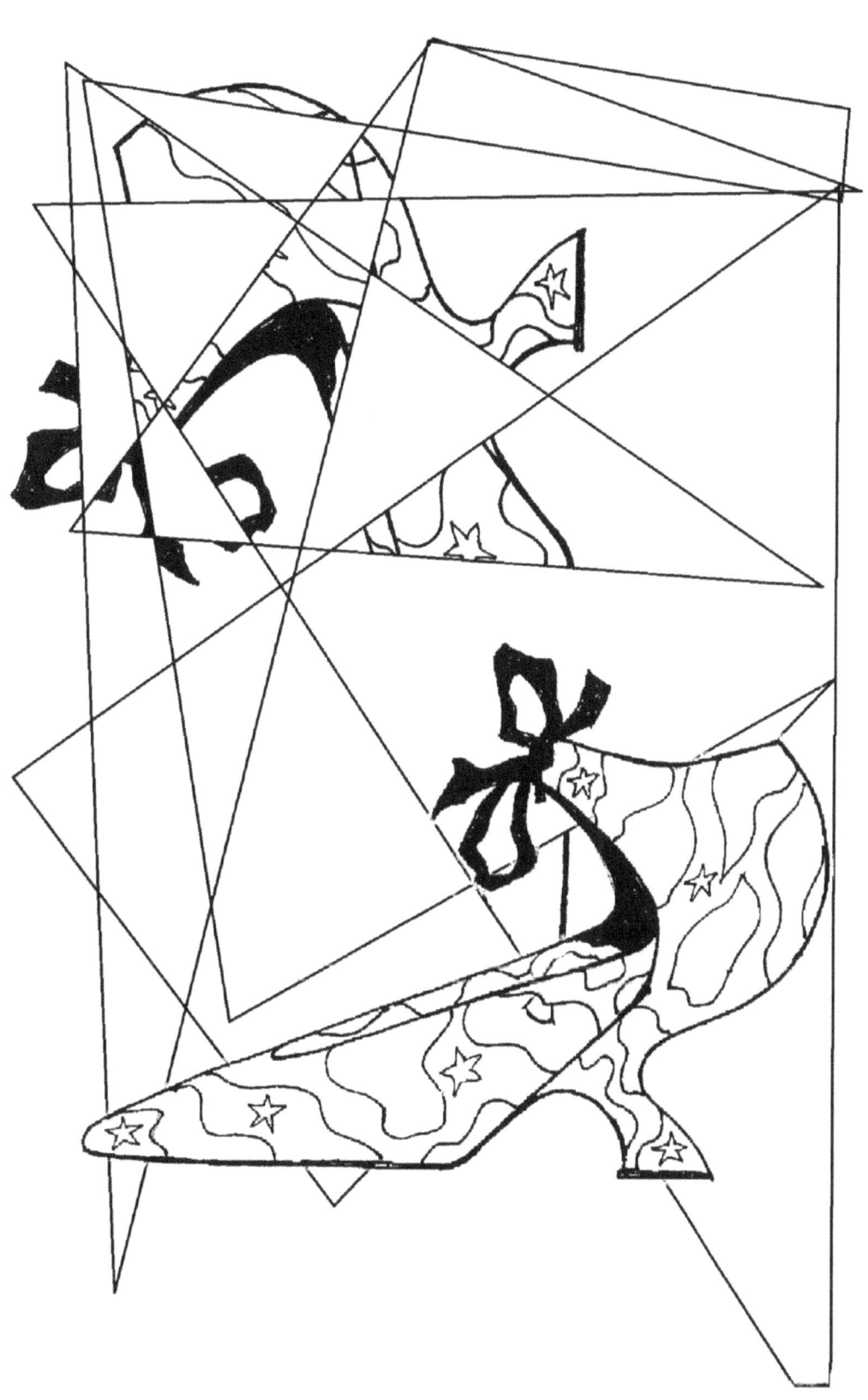

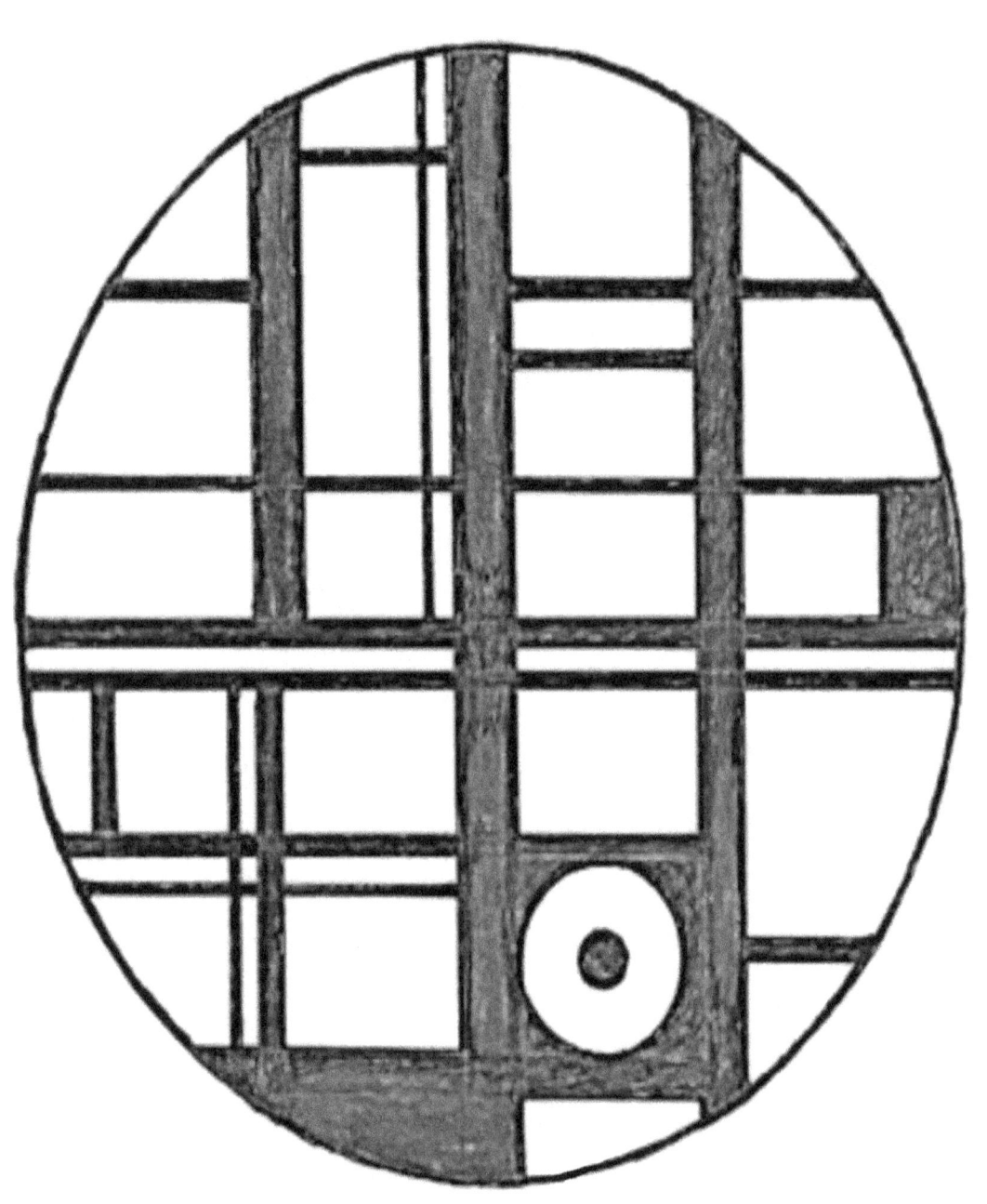

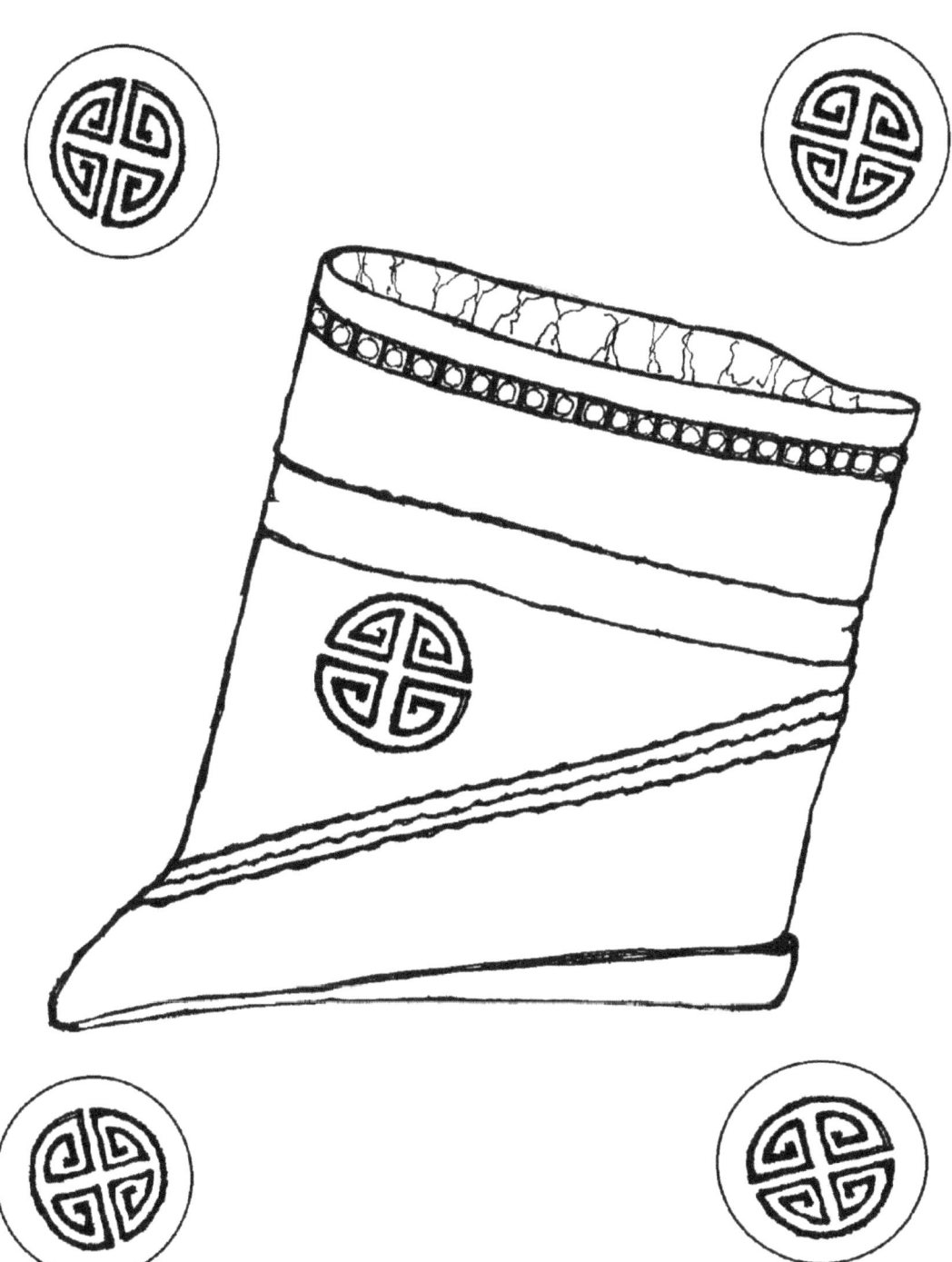

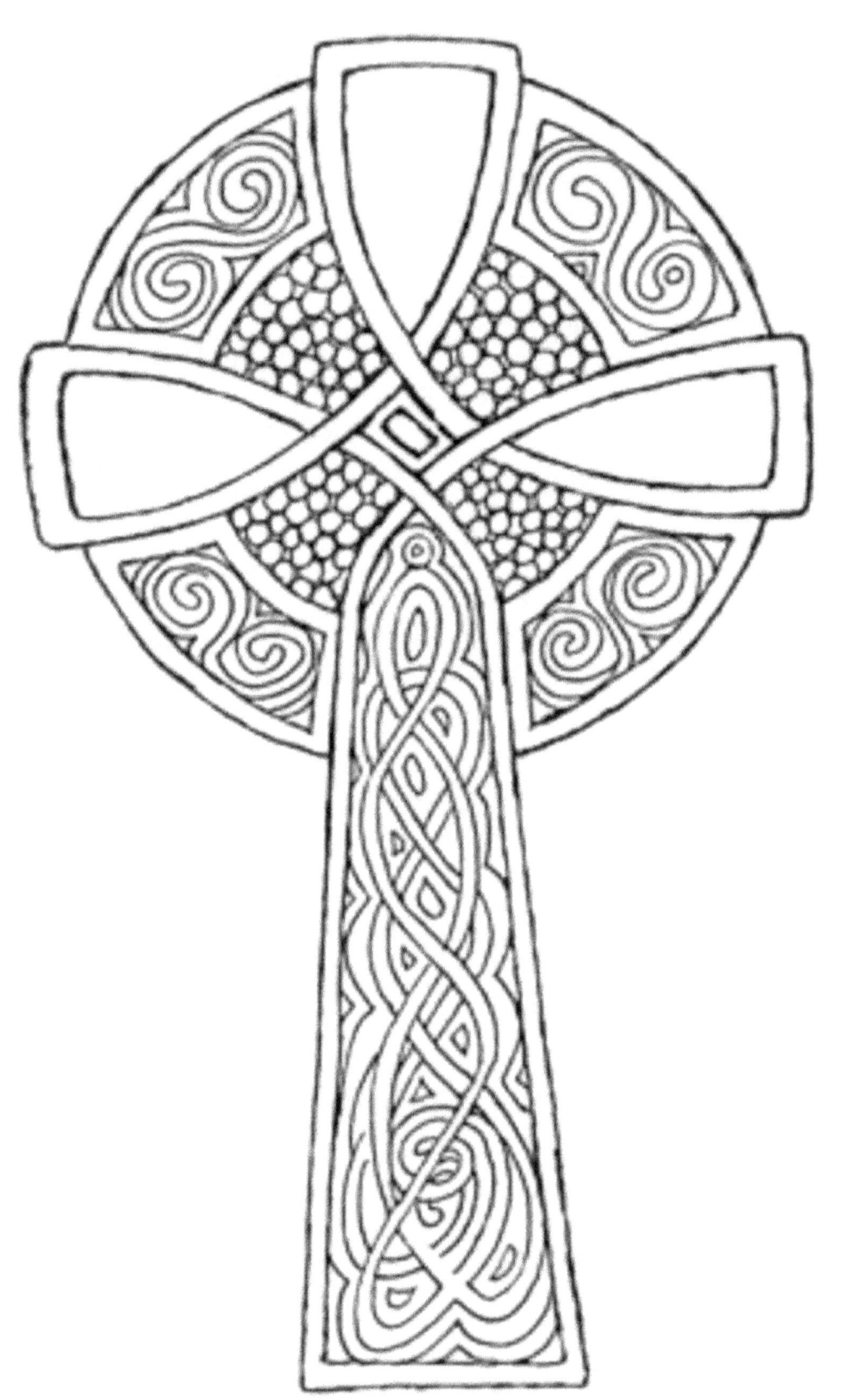

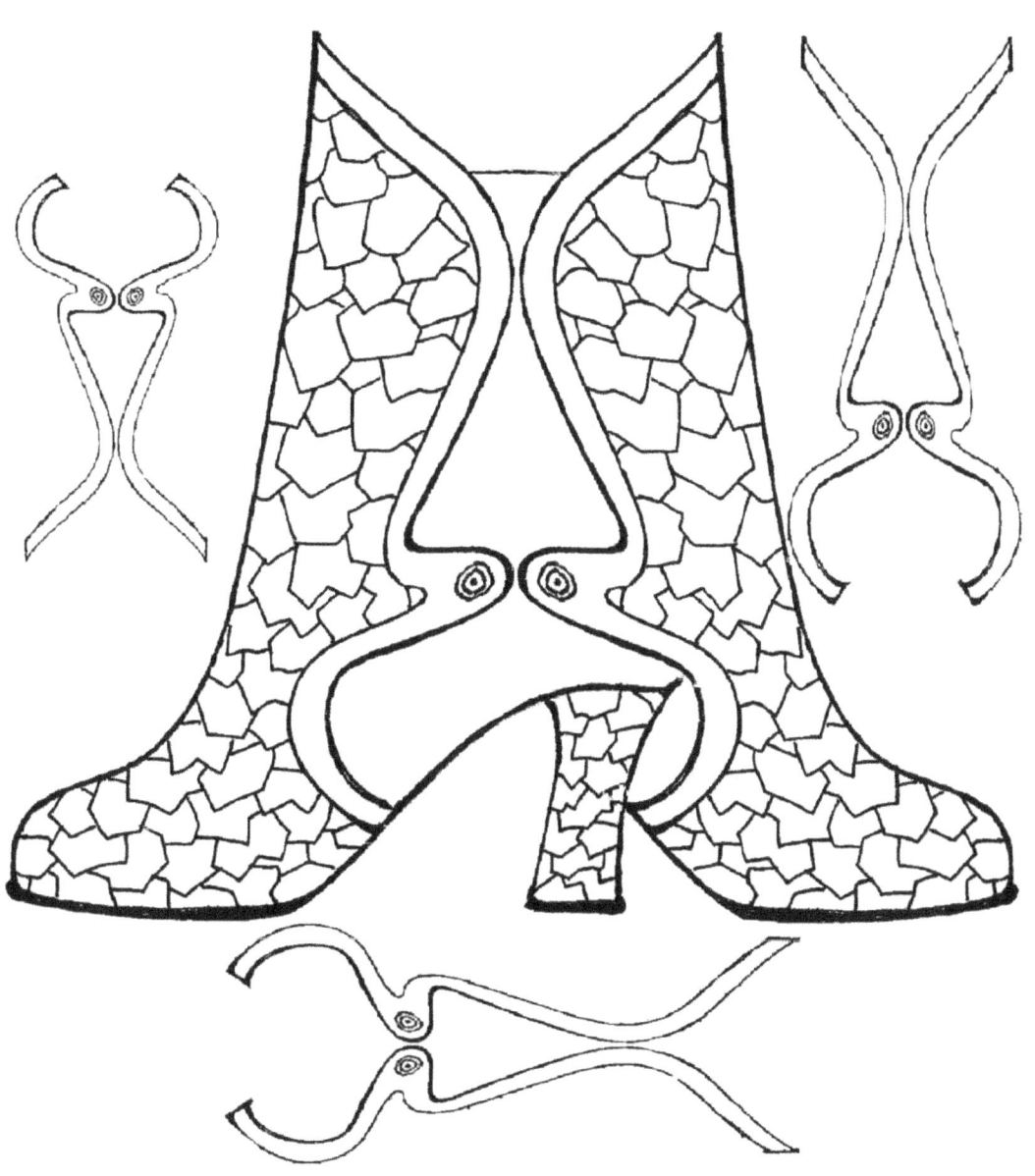

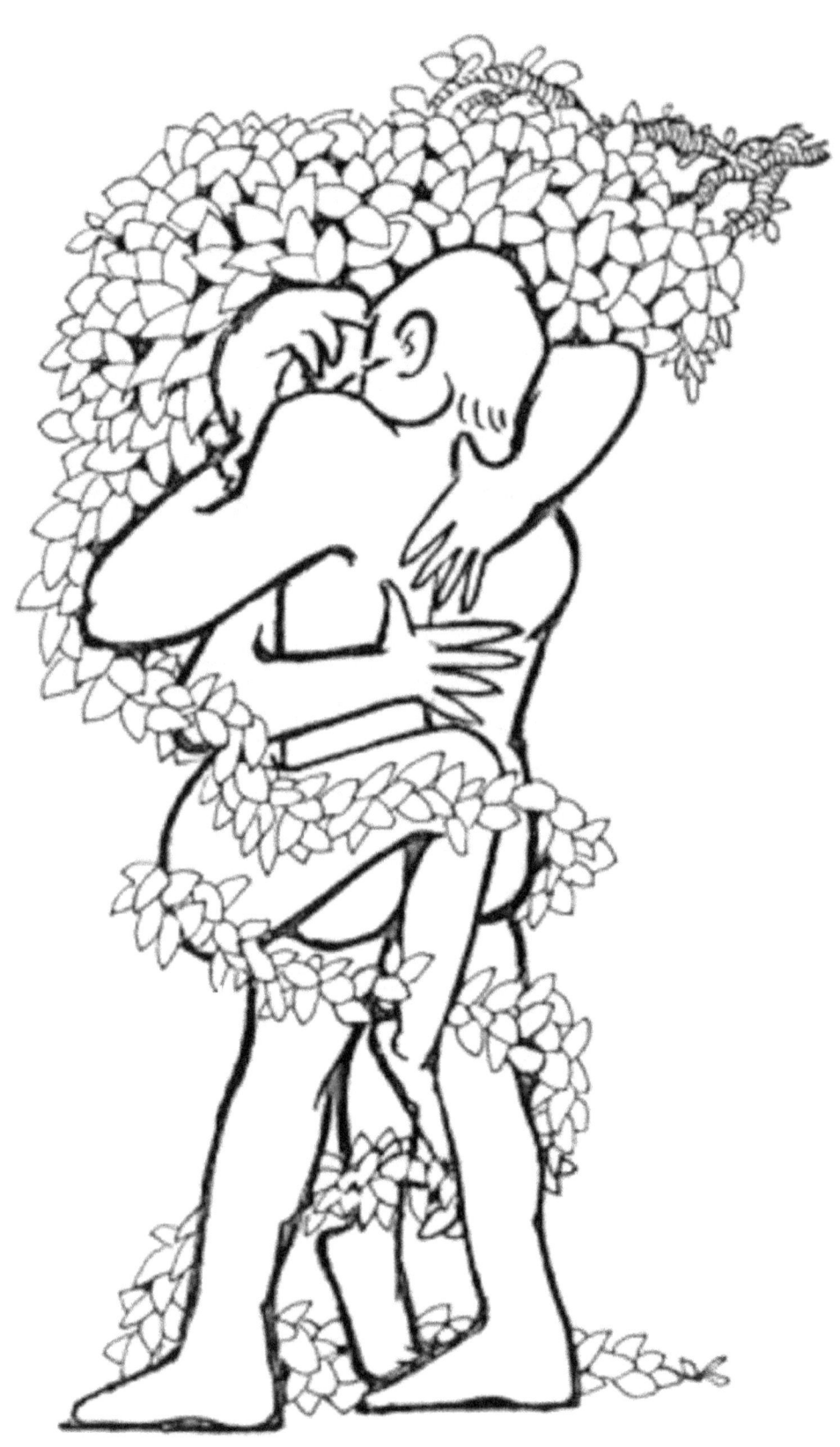

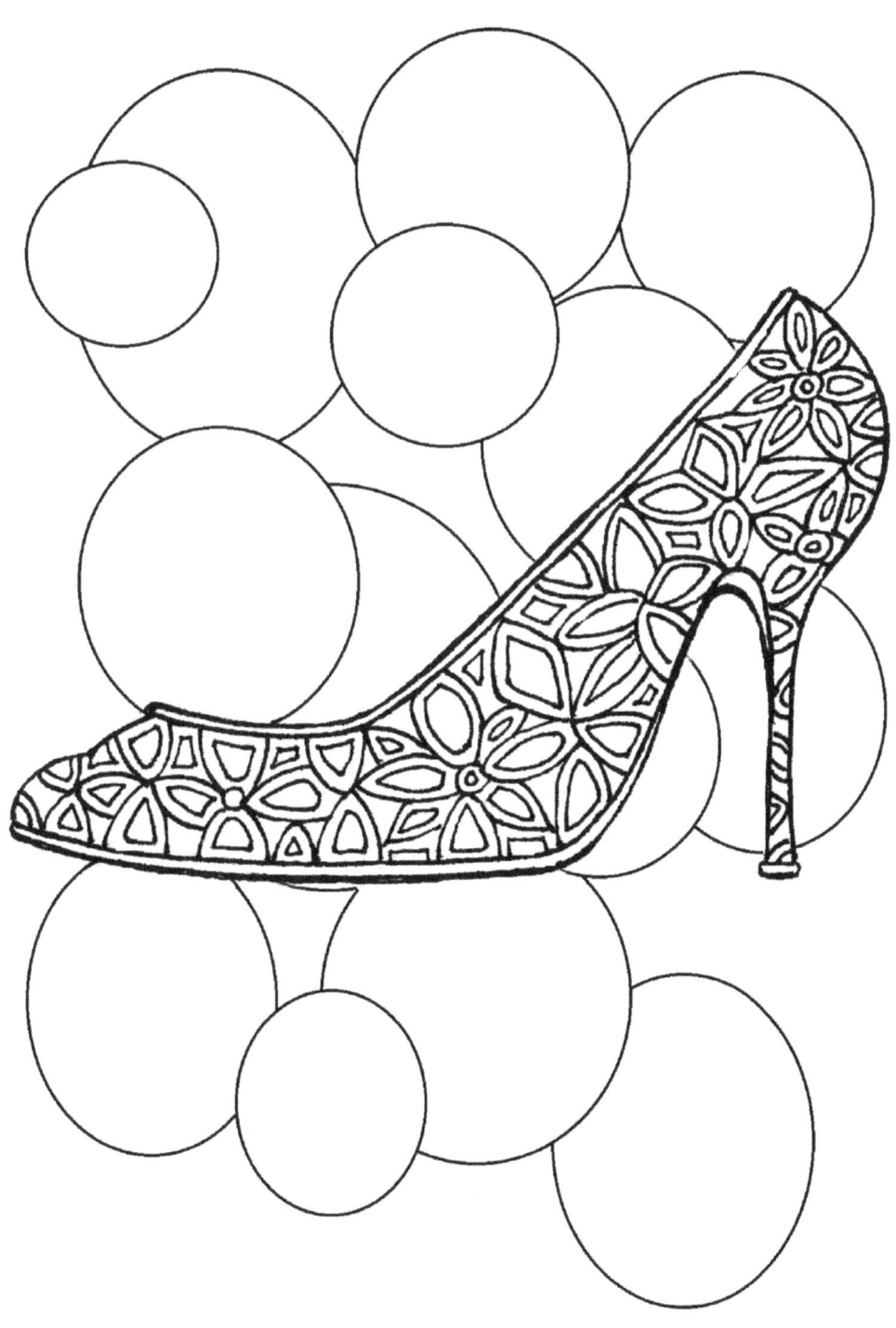

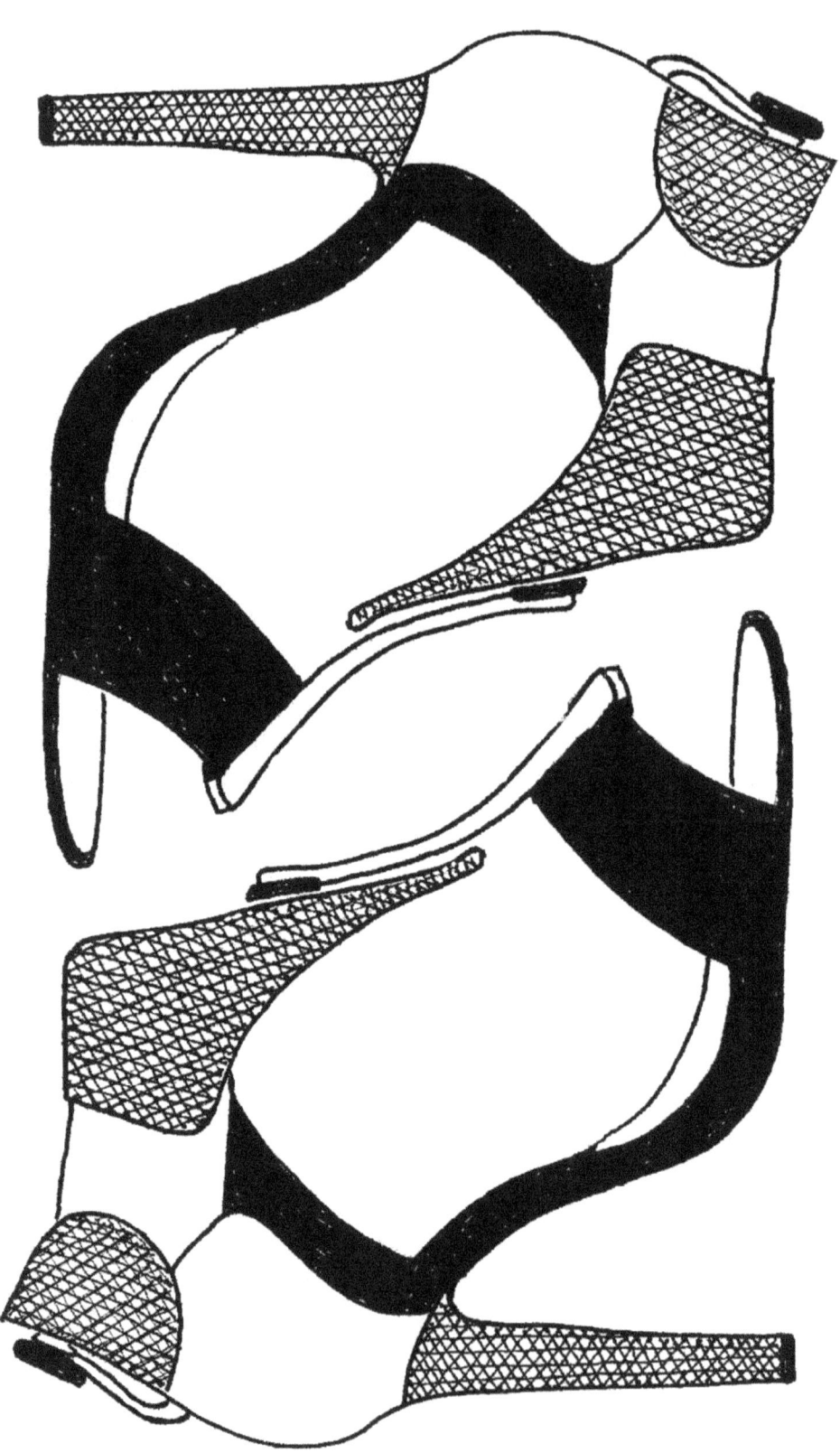

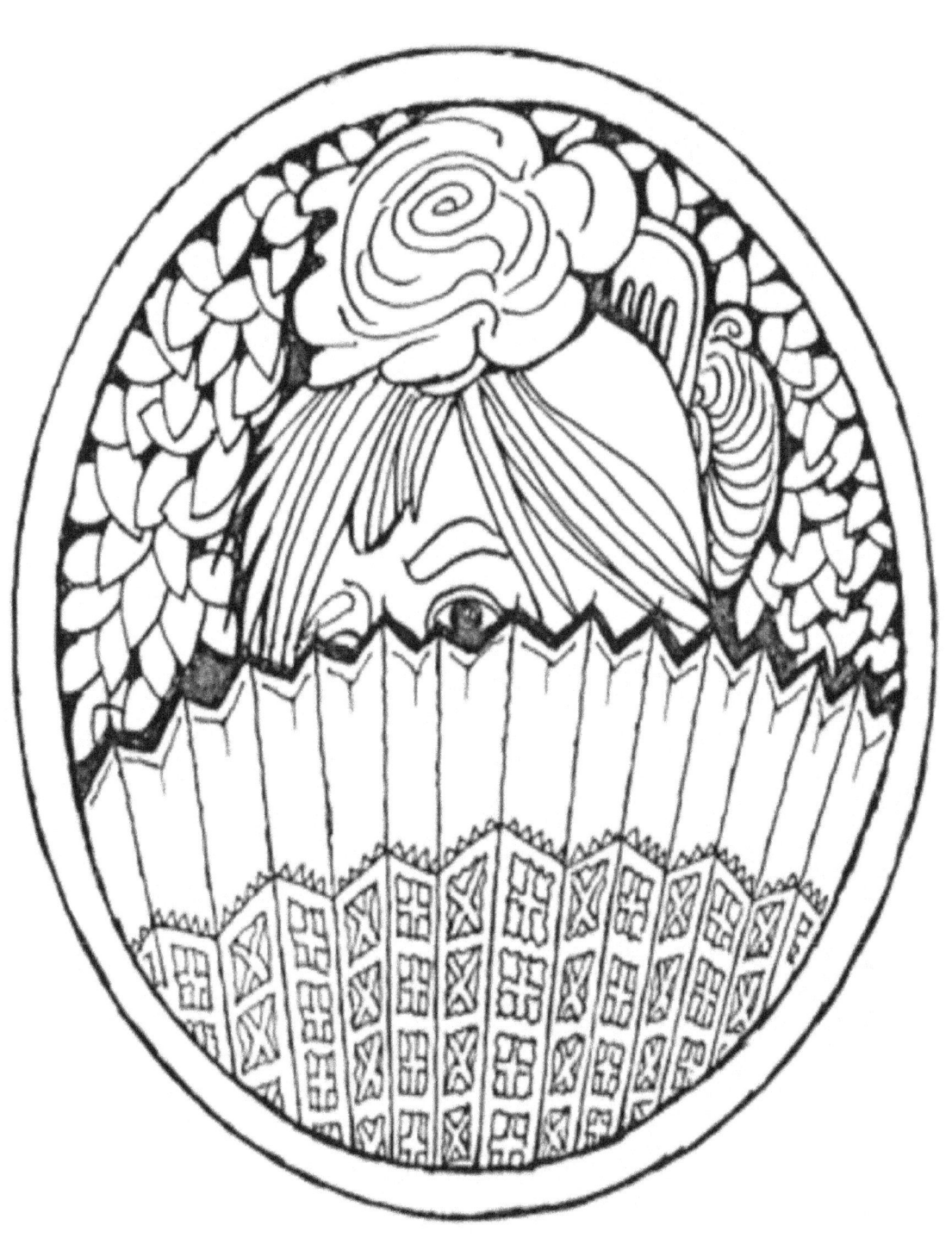

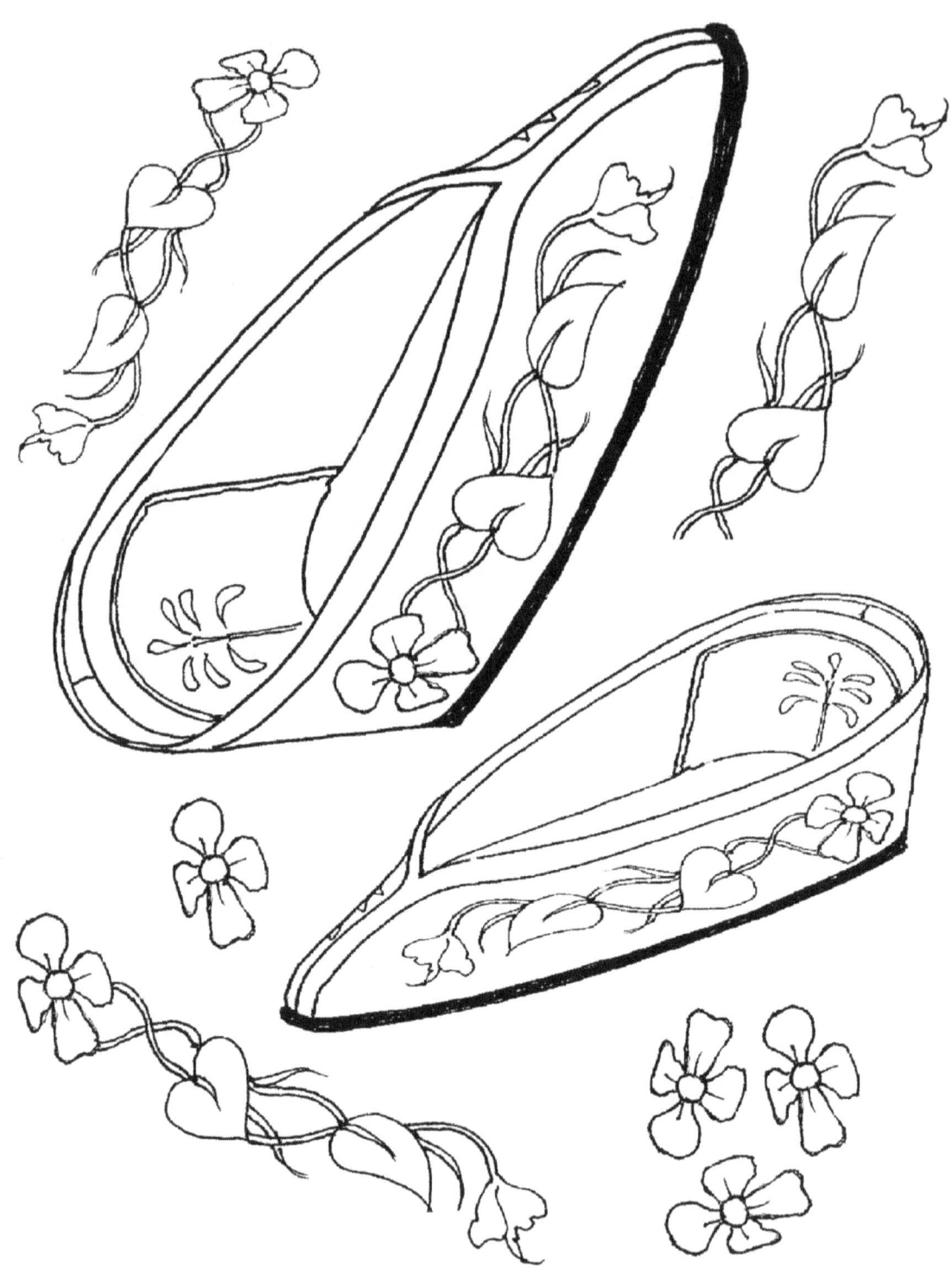

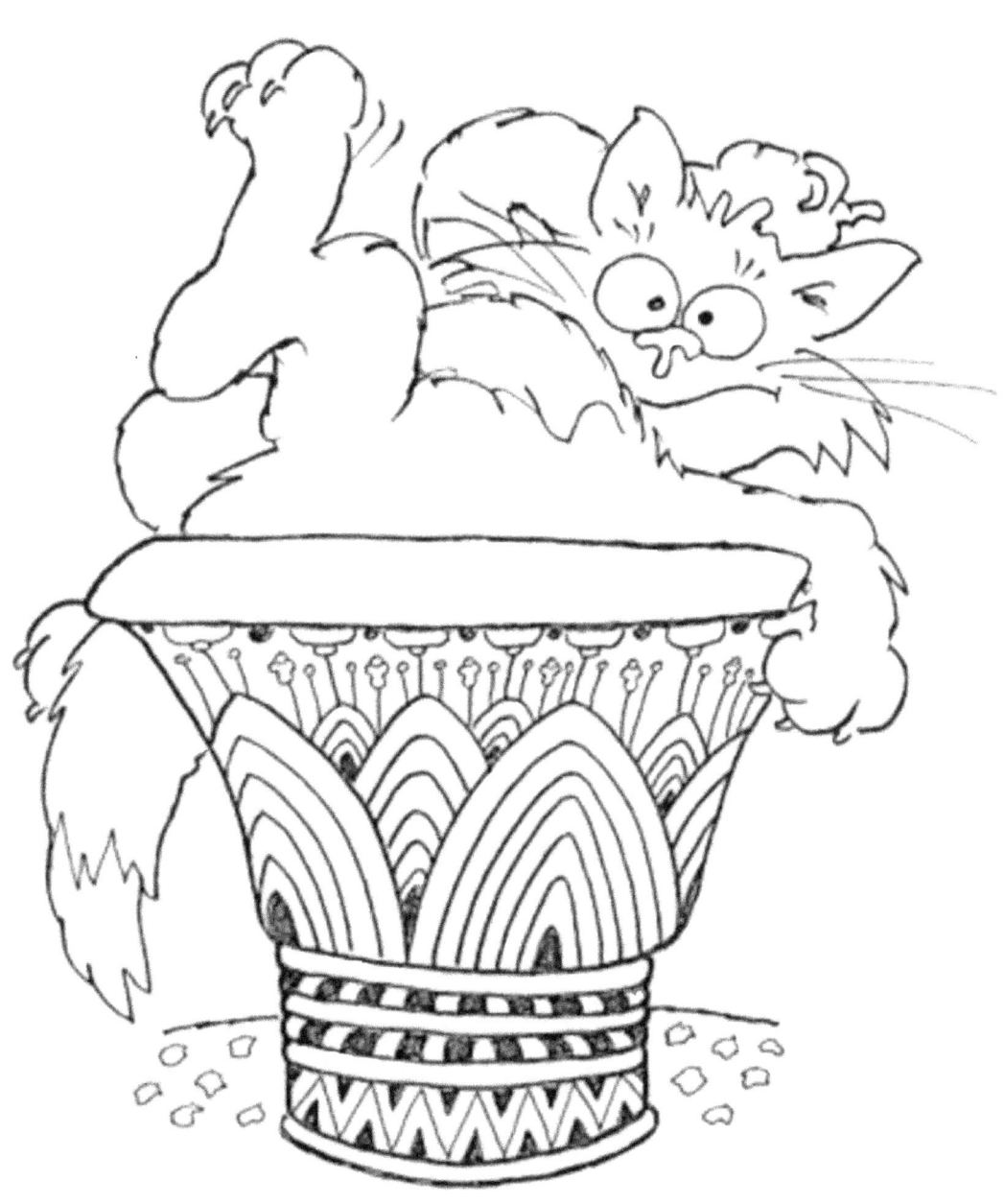

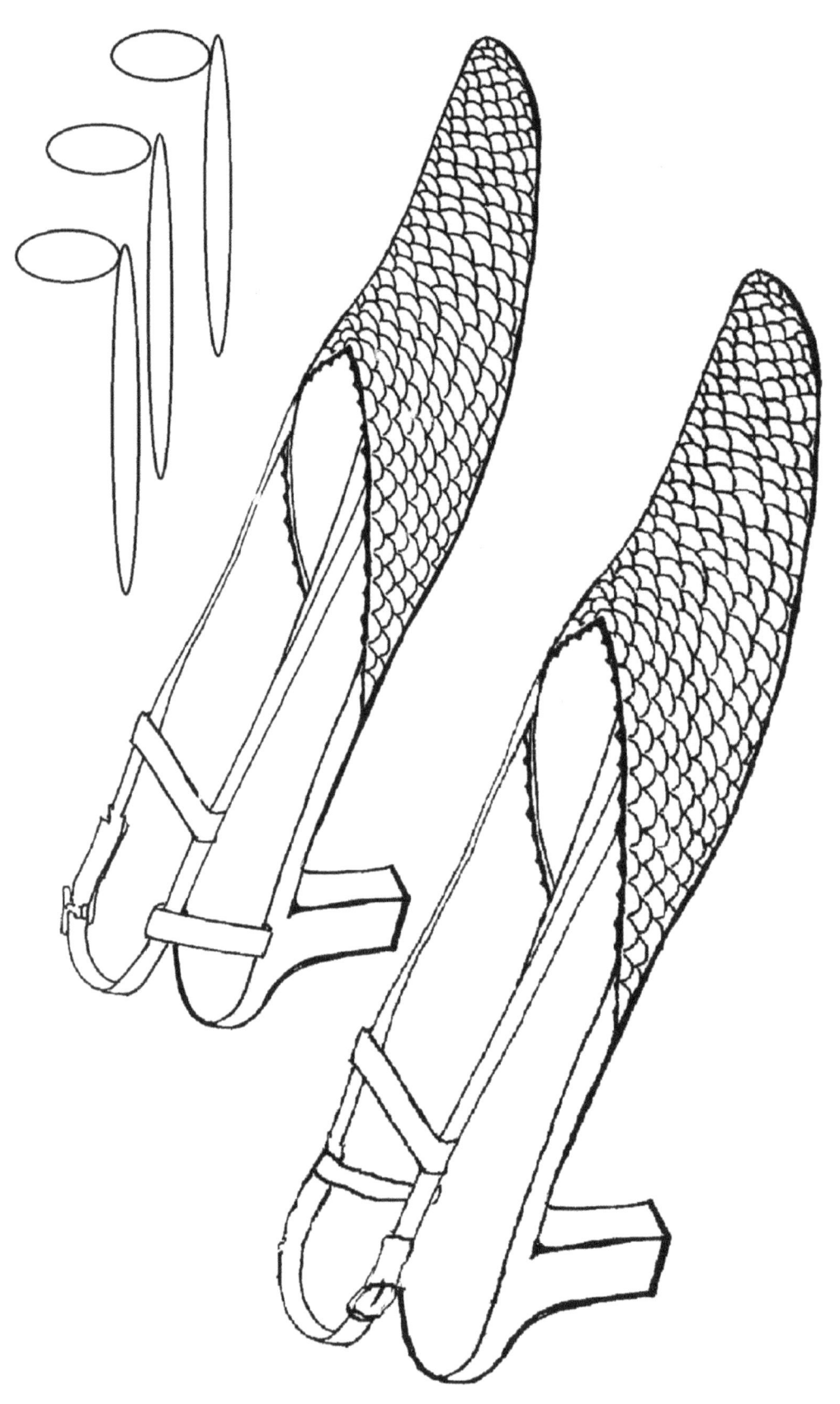

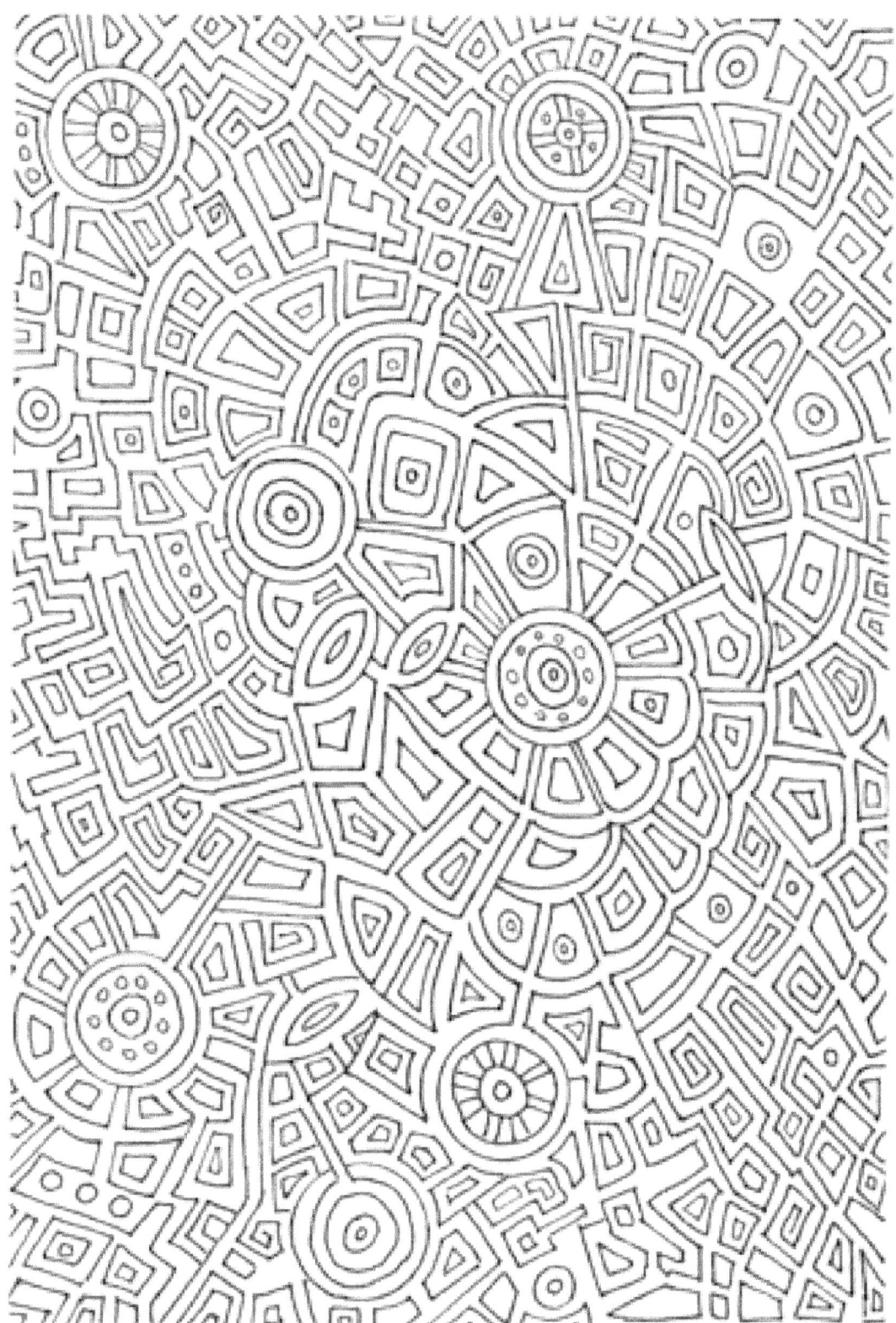

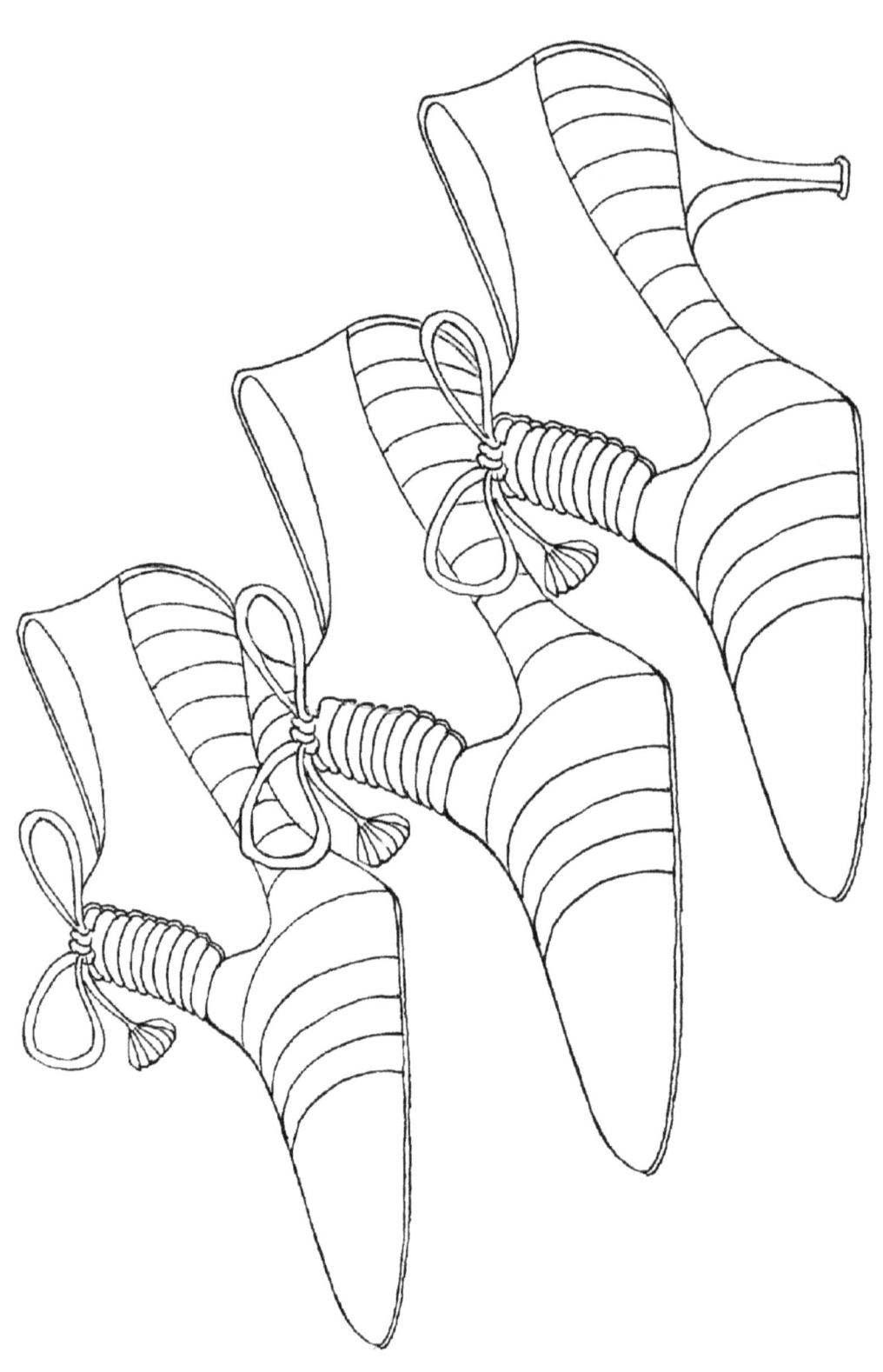

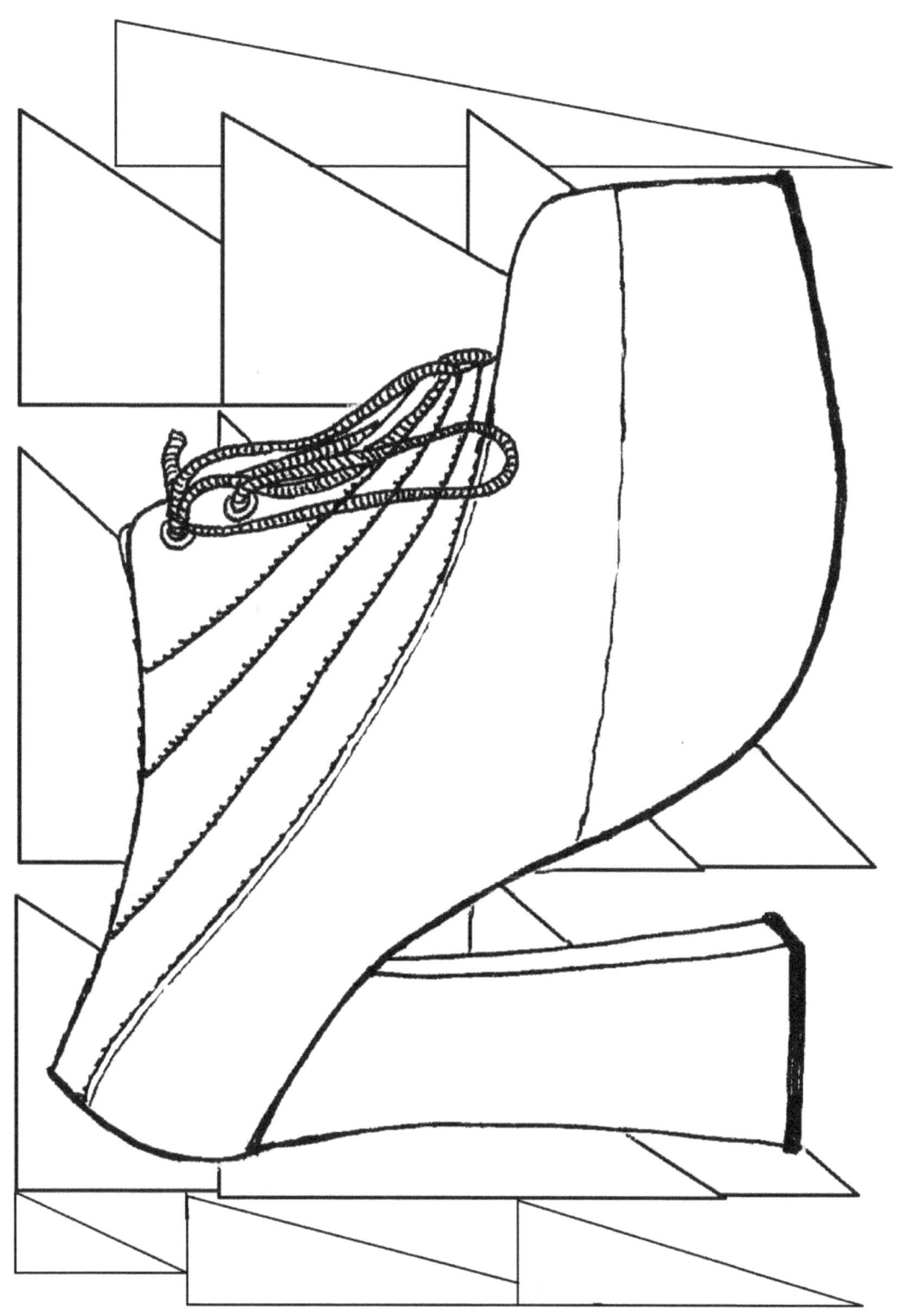

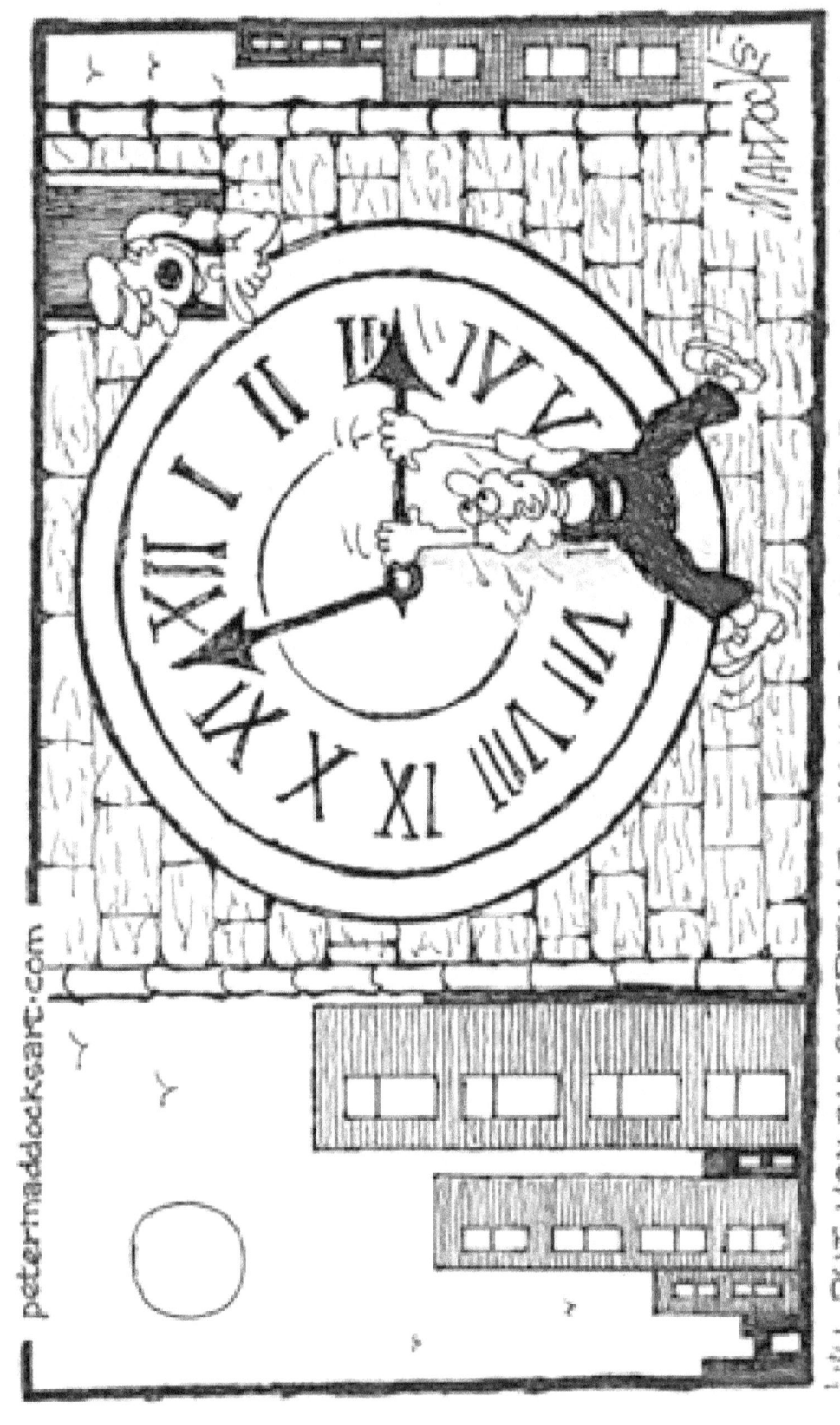

'I'LL PUT YOU ON OVERTIME – HANG ON UNTIL THREE A.M. SUNDAY AND THEN PUT THE CLOCK FORWARD ONE HOUR!'

peternaddocksart.com

A little about the Author:

Peter Maddocks, Fleet Street Cartoonist, and children's filmmaker, now resides in southern Spain.

In 2011 he began to release his many 'How to draw books' in several different languages; Short stories for children, and a whole new collection of stories for adults, in eBook and paperback!

He spends a great deal of his time drawing, and painting in his many styles. Please find examples of his work at:

petermaddocksart.com
PublishedByMe.Blogspot.com

www.ingramcontent.com/pod-product-compliance
Lightning Source LLC
Chambersburg PA
CBHW080647180526
45168CB00008B/3330